EASY
Tagalog

Learn to Speak Tagalog Quickly!

DISCARD

Joi Barrios and Julia Camagong

TUTTLE Publishing

Tokyo | Rutland, Vermont | Singapore

The Tuttle Story: "Books to Span the East and West"

Many people are surprised to learn that the world's leading publisher of books on Asia had humble beginnings in the tiny American state of Vermont. The company's founder, Charles E. Tuttle, belonged to a New England family steeped in publishing.

Immediately after WWII, Tuttle served in Tokyo under General Douglas MacArthur and was tasked with reviving the Japanese publishing industry. He later founded the Charles E. Tuttle Publishing Company, which thrives today as one of the world's leading independent publishers.

Though a westerner, Tuttle was hugely instrumental in bringing a knowledge of Japan and Asia to a world hungry for information about the East. By the time of his death in 1993, Tuttle had published over 6,000 books on Asian culture, history and art—a legacy honored by the Japanese emperor with the "Order of the Sacred Treasure," the highest tribute Japan can bestow upon a non-Japanese.

With a backlist of 1,500 titles, Tuttle Publishing is more active today than at any time in its past—still inspired by Charles Tuttle's core mission to publish fine books to span the East and West and provide a greater understanding of each.

Published by Tuttle Publishing, an imprint of Periplus Editions (HK) Ltd.

www.tuttlepublishing.com

Copyright © Periplus Editions (HK) Ltd.
Cover photo © William Casey and Tyler Olson/fotolia

Library of Congress Cataloging-in-Publication Data is in process.

ISBN: 978-0-8048-4314-0

First edition
18 17 16 15   5 4 3 2 1   1504MP

Printed in Singapore

Distributed by

North America, Latin America & Europe
Tuttle Publishing
364 Innovation Drive, North Clarendon,
VT 05759-9436, USA
Tel: 1 (802) 773 8930;
Fax: 1 (802) 773 6993
info@tuttlepublishing.com
www.tuttlepublishing.com

Asia Pacific
Berkeley Books Pte Ltd
61 Tai Seng Avenue #02-12
Singapore 534167
Tel: (65) 6280 1330;
Fax: (65) 6280 6290
inquiries@periplus.com.sg
www.periplus.com

Contents

INTRODUCTION 5

CHAPTER 1 How are you?
Kumusta ka? 9

CHAPTER 2 Where are you from?
Taga–saan ka? 19

CHAPTER 3 What is your job?
Ano ang trabaho mo? 31

CHAPTER 4 What is your mother's name?
Ano ang pangalan ng nanay mo? 43

CHAPTER 5 Where is our cat, Muning?
Nasaan si Muning, ang ating pusa? 53

CHAPTER 6 Do you have a pen?
May bolpen ka ba? 61

CHAPTER 7 How many pens do you have?
Ilan ang bolpen mo? 75

CHAPTER 8 Would you like some coffee?
Gusto mo ba ng kape? 89

CHAPTER 9 Can I open a checking account?
Puwede po ba akong magbukas ng checking account? 105

CHAPTER 10 What is the exchange rate?
Magkano ang palitan ng pera? 115

CHAPTER 11 What time is it?
Anong oras na?......................125

CHAPTER 12 What time do you eat breakfast?
Anong oras ka nag-aalmusal?......................137

CHAPTER 13 What would you like to eat?
Ano ang gusto mong kainin?......................147

CHAPTER 14 Can you take me to the doctor?
Puwede mo ba akong samahan sa doktor......................161

CHAPTER 15 What is the weather like on Saturday?
Ano ang lagay ng panahon sa Sabado?......................173

CHAPTER 16 Can I rent this apartment?
Puwede ko bang upahan ang apartment na ito?..........189

CHAPTER 17 Where are you going? **Saan ka pupunta?**................203

CHAPTER 18 What time does the bus leave?
Anong oras umaalis ang bus?......................215

CHAPTER 19 Can you take me to the shopping mall?
Puwede n'yo ba akong dalhin sa shopping mall?..........225

CHAPTER 20 What shall I wear to the party?
Ano ang isusuot ko sa party?......................235

GRAMMAR INDEX......................249
ENGLISH-TAGALOG GLOSSARY......................250
TAGALOG-ENGLISH GLOSSARY......................ON DISC
AUDIO TRACKLIST......................INSIDE FRONT COVER

Introduction

Designed for individual learners, **Easy Tagalog** has 20 short lessons. The book focuses on basic vocabulary, practical situations, and grammar needs, in an easy-to-follow way: it forms a step-by-step guide towards building sentences and dialogues.

The focus is conversational: there are 2 or 3 dialogues per lesson, and all dialogues are short so that they can easily be remembered as you build your skills.

The dialogues follow two characters, both travelling to the Philippines for the first time: Melissa Roja, a 20-year old Filipina American student studying at the University of the Philippines; and Ralph Woods, a bank manager on a two-year assignment for North American Investment Bank. Melissa is staying at the house of her cousin Sarah, an advertising executive, and Ralph is renting a condominium unit in Makati. A fourth character is Mr. Richard Tolentino, a lawyer at Ralph's bank.

The sidebars Info boxes throughout offer two kinds of tips: *grammar tips* and *culture tips*. At the end of each lesson, you'll find a place to pause, and to "sum up" what you've covered, usually by creating a few sentences.

What are some tips you need to remember as a Tagalog language learner?

First, do not get confused with the name of the language. Some people may refer to it as Tagalog, Pilipino, or Filipino. Tagalog is the name of the language of the ethnolinguistic group, the Tagalogs, living in what is now known as the Metro Manila area, as well as provinces in Central and Southern Luzon (Aurora, Bataan, Batangas, Bulacan, Cavite, Laguna, Marinduque, Nueva Ecija, Mindoro, Quezon, Rizal and Zambales). Pilipino is based on Tagalog, and it was the name designated by the Department of Education when it called for the teaching of a national language in 1959. With the designation of a national language based on Tagalog in 1936, the letter k (from the indigenous system of writing, the *baybayin*), was reinstated in the standardized alphabet created in 1940. Filipino was the term given to the national language by the 1987 constitution and it included the letters c, f, j, ñ, q, v, x, and z, which were not used in Pilipino.

Second, the key to language learning is honing the ability to express yourself. As you study each lesson, you may notice that we have given emphasis to two kinds of exercises: questions and answers and role-play situations. We would like you to practice asking and answering questions and to be able to use what you are learning from this book in real-life situations.

Third, remember that most Filipinos speak in what is called Taglish or Tagalog-English. Do not rack your brains trying to think of Tagalog equivalents to words like computer, hamburger, bus, school, grocery etc. You can use these words in your Filipino sentences. The important thing is that people understand what you are saying.

Fourth, use Tagalog word formation to your advantage. In Tagalog, words are formed through root (or base) words and affixes. For verbs, among the affixes used are **mag-** (with its variation **nag-**) and **um-**. If at a loss for a verb, for example, **langoy** (*swim*), simply say, "**Nag-swimming ako!**" (*I went swimming!*).

Fifth, do not be afraid of making grammatical mistakes or having the wrong pronunciation. Even native speakers make grammatical mistakes. Just try your best to speak the language and people will appreciate you.

Tagalog is not the easiest language to learn, but neither is it the most difficult. We tried to make this book easy to follow and a practical one to use.

As with other book writers, there are people we would like to acknowledge—foremost among them, Nancy and Pat, for their guidance and patience and our college friend Ralph Peña, for his unwavering friendship in our site of migration.

Joi Barrios dedicates this book to her foster parents Bien and Shayne Lumbera, her husband Pierre and her son Elia. She also thanks the following for providing assistance in research, proofreading and the making of the glossary and index: Jan Tristan Gaspi, Althea Contreras, Raphael Bernabe, Abigail Ong, and Allen Siapno.

Julia Camagong dedicates this book to her parents Fely and Ben Camagong, her daughter Renia Gardner, and Robert Roy—for their unconditional love and support. She also thanks the following for their assistance in recording the dialogues, guidance and support: Joanne Beshansky, Philippine Forum, College of Mount Saint Vincent, Potri Ranka Manis, Jonna Baldres, Ramon Mappala, Rusty Fabunan, Cling Corotan, Michelle Saulon, Melanie Dulfo, Yancy Gandionco, Rey Agudana, Gary Labao and Noel Pangilinan.

Joi Barrios
Julia Camagong

EASY
Tagalog

CHAPTER 1

How are you?
Kumusta ka?

Ralph Woods, a bank manager on a two-year assignment in Manila for the North American Investment Bank is at a party hosted by one of his Filipino friends. He is meeting Sarah, an advertising company executive.

Introductions

Let us learn about introducing oneself. Here are some words, phrases, and sentences.

Kumusta ka?	*How are you?* (informal; derived from the Spanish "Como esta?")
ka	*You* (second person singular)
Mabuti	*Fine.*
ako	*I* (first person singular)
si	subject marker (This word tells us that the word which follows it is the subject of the sentence. It is used for proper nouns or names.)
Ako si Sarah.	I + **si** + Sarah. *I am Sarah.*
ang	subject marker (This word tells us that the word which follows it is the subject of the sentence. It is used for common nouns.)
pangalan ko	*name*
	my (first person singular, possessive); *I* (first person singular)
Ralph ang pangalan ko.	Ralph + **ang** + name + my. *My name is Ralph.*
Ikinagagalak	*pleased*
ikinagagalak ko	*I am pleased*
na	linker (used to link words; used here to mean the word "to)"
kong	contraction of **ko** + **na**
makilala	*meet*
Ikinagagalak kong makilala ka.	Pleased + I + **na** (used for *to*) + meet + you. *Pleased to meet you.*

Study this dialogue to learn how to introduce yourself in Tagalog.

RALPH : **Kumusta ka?** *How are you?*
SARAH : **Mabuti. Ako si Sarah.** *Fine. I am Sarah.*
RALPH : **Ralph Woods ang pangalan ko.** *My name is Ralph Woods.*
SARAH : **Ikinagagalak* kong makilala ka.** *Pleased to meet you.*
RALPH : **Ikinagagalak kong makilala ka.** *Pleased to meet you.*

Note: ikinagagalak is pronounced /ikinAgAgA'lak/ with the stress on the fourth syllable.

Now practice the dialogue.

SENTENCE CONSTRUCTION

Let's study the following words and how to formulate questions.

Sino	*Who*
Sino ka?	Who + you? *Who are you?*
po	honorific; used to show politeness and respect
kayo	*you* (plural)
Sino po kayo?	Who + honorific + you?
	Who are you? (formal; polite)
ano	*what*

Ano ang pangalan mo? What + **ang** + name + your? *What is your name?*

There is no equivalent of the verb "to be" (are, is) in Tagalog. Thus, if you look at "**Sino ka?**" the literal translation is just "Who you?" Similarly, the literal translation for **Ano ang pangalan mo?** is "What marker name your?"

A brief culture note – the question "**Sino ka?**" is not considered to be polite. Unless you are speaking to someone much younger, it is best to use **Sino po kayo?**

Let's study how to answer these questions. One important characteristic of the Tagalog language is flexibility. We can change the order of the sentence. The subject (person, place, thing, or idea of doing something) can come before the predicate (tells something about the subject), or the predicate can come before the subject.

In Tagalog, the predicate–subject order is more commonly used, especially in conversations. The subject–predicate order is considered formal and less common. Thus, it is called an "inverted order" by grammarians. Here are two ways to construct sentences.

Question: **Sino po kayo?** *Who are you?*

	Predicate–Subject	Subject–Predicate
Answers:	**Si Sarah ako.**	**Ako si Sarah.**
	Si +Sarah + I. (*Sarah I.*)	I + **si** + Sarah. (*I Sarah.*)
		I am Sarah.

Question: **Ano ang pangalan mo?** *What is your name?*

	Predicate–Subject	Subject–Predicate
Answers:	**Ralph ang pangalan ko.**	**Ang pangalan ko ay Ralph.**
	Ralph + **ang** + name + my.	**Ang** + name + my + **ay** + Ralph.
		My name is Ralph.

Note: The word **ay**—Some learners get confused and think that this is the verb "to be" and is the equivalent of the words *am*, or *is*. According to Tagalog grammar, **ay** is actually a particle (minor function word) that serves as a linker (used to connect the subject and the predicate).

Now, practice asking and answering questions.

QUESTION AND ANSWER PRACTICE

Now, let us practice some of the words you learned by asking and answering questions:

1. Question: **Kumusta ka?**

   Answer: _____.

2. Question: **Ano ang pangalan mo?**

   Answer: _____.

3. Question: _____?

   Answer: **Mabuti.**

4. Question: _____?

   Answer: **Sarah ang pangalan ko.**

> **LANGUAGE AND CULTURE TIP (Tongue-Twisters):** Ikinagagalak kong makilala **ka** is a tongue-twister. It also sounds very formal. If you forget it, don't let this bother you. Just plunge into the conversation by saying your name, and then say "**Kumusta ka?**" You'll be fine.

Introducing Oneself to an Older Person

At the same party, Ralph later meets Mr. Tolentino, a lawyer. Mr. Tolentino is in his late 40s, and is older than Ralph. Thus, Ralph greets him politely, using the honorific words **po** and **pong**, and plural pronouns.

Here are a few words for polite speech and more pronouns.

pong contraction of the honorific **po** + **na** (linker)
ho honorific; used to show politeness and respect; less formal than **po**
ikaw *you* (second person singular; used only either alone or at the beginning of a sentence)
kayo *you* (second person plural)

Study how polite language is used.

 **DIALOGUE B**

RALPH   : **Kumusta po kayo?** *How are you?*
MR. TOLENTINO : **Mabuti. Ikaw?** *Fine. And you?*
RALPH   : **Mabuti po. Ako ho si Ralph.** *Fine. I am Ralph.*
MR. TOLENTINO : **Ako si Richard Tolentino.** *I am Richard Tolentino.*
RALPH   : **Ikinagagalak ko pong makilala kayo.** *Pleased to meet you.*
MR. TOLENTINO : **Ikinagagalak kong makilala ka.** *Pleased to meet you.*

Practice using polite language when introducing yourself.

GRAMMAR

Using Honorifics

You have learned two words that express politeness and respect: **po** and **ho**. While **po** is considered to be more formal than **ho**, these two words are interchangeable in conversations.

In general, **po/ho** is inserted after the first word of a sentence. For example,

Ako po si Ralph.	*I am Ralph.*
Ralph po ang pangalan ko.	*My name is Ralph.*
Ano po ang pangalan ninyo?	*What is your name?*

However, there are two exceptions.

* First, when the pronoun **ko** (singular object pronoun *I*) follows the verb, **po** is placed after **ko**. For example, **Ikinagagalak ko pong makilala kayo.** *Pleased to meet you.*

* Second, when **po** follows a set phrase used together, we put **po** after the full greeting instead of inserting it between **magandang** and **gabi**. For example, **Magandang gabi po** (*Good evening* po).

Pronouns

In the dialogues above, pronouns were introduced. Here is a chart of subject pronouns and singular possessive pronouns. Other pronouns will be introduced in later chapters.

	Singular subject pronouns	Plural subject pronouns	Singular possessive pronouns
1st person	**ako**	**kami** (exclusive) *us* **tayo** (inclusive) *us* or *we + you*	**ko** *my*
2nd person	**Ikaw, ka** *you*	**kayo** *you*	**mo** *your*
3rd person	**siya** *he/she*	**sila** *they*	**niya** *your* his

Here are some reminders for using Tagalog pronouns:

1. Use **ikaw** only at the beginning of a sentence. Elsewhere, use **ka**. They mean the same thing.

2. When using **po**, use the second person plural pronoun **kayo** and not **ka**. For example, "**Kumusta po kayo?**" and not "**Kumusta po ka?**"

3. There are two pronouns that are the equivalent of the English first person plural subject pronoun "us." One is **kami**. This is called an "exclusive" pronoun because it refers only to the people speaking and not to the person or people being addressed. The second is **tayo**. This is called an "inclusive" pronoun because it refers to everyone—the people speaking and the people being addressed.

Study the following sentence patterns.

Ako si Ralph.	I + **si** + Ralph. *I am Ralph.*
Ikaw si Sarah.	You + **si** + Sarah. (*You Sarah.*)
Si Sarah ka.	**Si** + Sarah + you. *You are Sarah.*
Siya si Mr. Tolentino.	He + **si** + Mr. Tolentino. *He is Mr. Tolentino.*

Here are some examples of sentences with possessive pronouns. The pronouns **ko, mo,** and **niya** always follow the word they modify—**pangalan** (*name*), in this case.

Ralph ang pangalan ko.	Ralph + **ang** + name + my. *My name is Ralph.*
Sarah ang pangalan mo.	Sarah + **ang** + name + your. *Your name is Sarah.*
Mr. Tolentino ang pangalan niya.	Mr. Tolentino + **ang** + name + **niya** + his. *His name is Mr. Tolentino.*

Let us learn words we can use to form sentences with plural subject pronouns.

mga (pronounced)/ mɐˈŋa/)	(used to make any common noun plural)
pangalan	*name*
mga pangalan	*names*
sina	subject marker for plural proper nouns
at	*and*
sina Ralph at Melissa	**sina** + Ralph + and + Melissa

To illustrate the difference between the plural pronouns **kami** (exclusive) and **tayo** (inclusive), let us study the following examples.

If Ralph and Melissa are speaking to Mr. Tolentino, they can say:

Kami sina Ralph at Melissa.	We (the speakers) + **sina** + Ralph + and + Melissa. *We are Ralph and Melissa.*
Tayo sina Ralph, Melissa, at Mr. Tolentino.	We (the speakers + person being addressed) + **sina** + Ralph + Melissa + and + Mr. Tolentino. *We are Ralph, Melissa, and Mr.Tolentino.*

QUESTION AND ANSWER PRACTICE

Answer and ask questions.

1. Question: **Ano ang pangalan mo?**

   Answer: _____ ang _____ ko.

2. Question: **Sino siya?**

   Answer: **Siya si** _____.

3. Question: **Ano** _____?

   Answer: **Mr. Tolentino ang pangalan niya.**

4. Question: **Ano ang** _____ **mo?**

   Answer: **Ako si Sarah.**

Introducing Another Person and Common Greetings

Now, let us study three things: common greetings, saying something about yourself/others, and introducing people.

Study the following words, phrases, and sentences to prepare for next dialogue.

ito	*this*
Ito si...	*this is ...*
Ito si Ralph.	This + **si** + Ralph. *This is Ralph.*
maganda	*beautiful; good*
magandang	contraction of **maganda** + **na**
gabi	*evening*
Magandang gabi!	Good + LINKER + **gabi** + evening. *Good evening!*
Magandang gabi po!	Good + LINKER + **gabi** + evening + **po**! *Good evening!*
din/rin	*also; too*
Magandang gabi rin.	Good + LINKER + evening + too. *Good evening too.*
estudyante	*student*
Estudyante siya.	Student + she. *She is a student.*

 **DIALOGUE C**

At the same party, Ralph meets Melissa, a student studying at the university of the Philippines. Melissa was brought to the party by her cousin, Sarah. Sarah is introducing Melissa to Ralph.

SARAH : **Melissa, ito si Ralph. Ralph, si Melissa. Estudyante siya.**
Melissa, this is Ralph. Ralph, Melissa. She is a student.

MELISSA : **Magandang gabi po.** *Good evening.*

RALPH : **Magandang gabi rin, Melissa.** *Good evening too, Melissa.*

Practice the dialogue above.

> **GRAMMAR AND CULTURE TIP (The letters D And R):** The words **din** and **rin** can be used to mean "also." The meaning of these words are exactly the same, but we use **din** when the preceding word ends with a consonant, and we use **rin** when the preceding word ends with a vowel. The interchangeability of letters "d" and "r" can be traced to the indigenous script **baybayin**, where these letters used the same symbol.

VOCABULARY

Here are other words you can use in greetings:

Magandang umaga!   *Good morning!*
Magandang tanghali!   *Good noon!* (literally)
Magandang hapon!   *Good afternoon!*
Magandang araw!   *Good day!*

PRACTICE EXERCISE

Study the following situations below. Note the time of day and the age or status of the person you are meeting. Greet this person.

1. You meet your classmate. It is 10:00 in the morning. You say:

   _____!

2. You meet your friend, who is about your age. It is 12:10 noon.
   You say: _____!

3. You meet your elderly neighbor while walking your dog. It is 7:00 in the evening.

   You say: _____!

4. You meet your aunt at a family gathering. It is 3:00 in the afternoon.

   You say: _____!

Saying Goodbye

To say goodbye, you can use the more formal word **paalam** or the more casual **sige** (which means both *goodbye* and *okay*).

DIALOGUE D

RALPH   : **Paalam, Melissa.** *Goodbye, Melissa.*
MELISSA : **Sige po.** *Bye.*

Practice saying goodbye.

SUMMING UP

In this chapter, we have studied greetings and introductions.

To sum up what we have learned, fill in the blanks. In the first sentence, you are talking about yourself. In the second sentence, you are talking to Ralph (remember to use the second person pronoun), and in the third, you are talking about Melissa.

Introduce yourself, Ralph, and Melissa to someone.

Ako si _____. _____ si Ralph _____

si Melissa. _____ si Melissa.

CHAPTER 2

Where are you from?
Taga–saan ka?

Ralph and Melissa are still at the party. They are talking about where they are from and where they are now living.

Then and Now

Study the following words, phrases and sentences that talk about places.

taga-saan	*from* (literally, *from-where*)
Taga-saan ka?	From-where + you? *Where are you from?*
taga-Los Angeles	*from-Los Angeles*
Taga-Los Angeles ako.	From-Los Angeles + I. *I am from Los Angeles.*
saan	*where*
nakatira	*living*
na	*already*
ngayon	*now*
Saan ka na nakatira ngayon?	Where + you + already + living + now? *Where do you live now?*
nakatira na ako ngayon	living + already + I + now. *I now live*
sa	*in* (preposition; can also mean *at* or *on*)
sa Quezon City	*in Quezon City.*
Nakatira na ako ngayon sa Quezon City.	Living + already + I + now + in + Quezon City. *I now live in Quezon City.*
noon	*in the past* or *previously*
Saan ka nakatira noon?	Where + you + live + previously? *Where did you live previously?*
Nakatira ako noon sa Manhattan.	Lived + I + previously + in + Manhattan. *I used to live in Manhattan.*

 **DIALOGUE A**

RALPH : **Taga-saan ka, Melissa?** *Where are you from, Melissa?*
MELISSA : **Taga-Los Angeles ako. Ikaw?** *I am from Los Angeles. And you?*
RALPH : **Taga-New York ako. Saan ka na nakatira ngayon?**
I am from New York. Where do you live now?
MELISSA : **Nakatira na ako sa Quezon City ngayon.**
I now live in Quezon City.

Practice this dialogue.

> **VOCABULARY AND CULTURE TIP (The word "Na")**: The word **na** has many meanings. In the dialogue, it is used to mean "already." In later chapters, it will be used as a linker (a word used to link adjectives with nouns), and as a relative pronoun (used to function as *who, whom, whose, which,* and *that*). Filipinos like to use the word "already." For example, they say "I ate already," instead of saying "I have eaten." This comes from the Tagalog sentence **Kumain na ako** (literally, *Ate already I.*) In English, using "already" would be wrong in a sentence like the one in the dialogue. Indeed it is a common source of mistakes when Filipinos are learning English.

QUESTION AND ANSWER PRACTICE

Read the information given in the following chart. The second column indicates where the person is from, and the third column shows where a person is living now. Use the third row to fill in your name, where you are from, and where you are living now, in each respective column. After doing this, ask and answer questions.

Person	Where they are from	Where they are living now
Sarah	**Pampanga**	**Maynila** (Manila)
Mr. Tolentino	**Nueva Ecija**	Makati City

1. Question: **Taga-saan si Sarah?**

   Answer: _____.

2. Question: **Saan na nakatira si Sarah ngayon?**

   Answer: _____.

3. Question: _____?

   Answer: Taga-Nueva Ecija si Mr. Tolentino.

4. Question: _____?

   Answer: Nakatira na siya sa Makati City ngayon.

5. Question: Taga-saan ka?

   Answer: _____.

6. Question: Saan ka na nakatira ngayon?

   Answer: _____.

VOCABULARY

Study the following words that describe location:

lugar	*place*
barangay	smallest political unit in the Philippines (similar to a village)
bayan	*town, country, people*
lungsod	*city*
probinsiya	*province*
isla	*island*
estado	*state*
bansa	*country*
kontinente	*continent*
mundo/daigdig	*world*
uniberso	*universe*

> **CULTURE TIP (The Word Bayan):** The word **bayan** can mean *town, country* and *people*. Here are some examples of how the word can be used: **bayan ng Santa Filomena** (*town of Filomena*); **bayang Pilipinas** (*country of the Philippines*); **maglingkod sa bayan** (*serve the people*). Historian Damon Woods has written about **bayan** in his book, *From Wilderness to Nation* (University of the Philippines, 2011).

SENTENCE CONSTRUCTION

In the beginning of this chapter, you learned the following:

Saan ka nakatira?   *Where do you live?*
Nakatira ako sa   *I live in Quezon City.*
  Quezon City.

Now, let us learn another *where* question: *Where is Quezon City?* To answer this question we need to learn another equivalent of the word *where:* **nasaan.**

nasaan	*where*
ng	*of* (can also mean *by, from,* and *with*; also used as an object marker)
lungsod ng Quezon	city + of + Quezon *city of Quezon* or *Quezon City*
Nasaan ang lungsod ng Quezon?	Where + **ang** + city + of + Quezon? *Where is the city of Quezon?*
nasa	*in* (can also mean *at* and *on*)
nasa Metro Manila	*in Metro Manila*
Nasa Metro Manila ang lungsod ng Quezon.	In + Metro Manila + **ang** + city + of Quezon. *The city of Quezon is in Metro Manila.*

Both **saan** and **nasaan** mean *where,* and both **sa** and **nasa** mean *in, at* and *on.* While these words have the same meaning, they differ in the usage:

1. Use **saan** only when there is a verb, for example, the verb **nakatira** (*living*) in **Saan ka nakatira?** (*Where do you live?*)

2. Use **nasaan** when it is followed by a noun, for example, **Nasaan ang Quezon City?** (*Where is Quezon City?*)

3. The prepositions **sa** and **nasa** have to match the question words. **Saan** questions should be answered by sentences with **sa,** and **nasaan** questions should be answered by sentences with **nasa.** Here are some examples:

Question: **Saan ka nakatira?** *Where do you live?*
Answer: **Nakatira ako sa Quezon City.** *I live in Quezon City.*
Question: **Nasaan ang Quezon City?** *Where is Quezon City?*
Answer: **Nasa Metro Manila ang Quezon City.** *Quezon City is in Metro Manila.*

Review the new words and sentence structures you have learned and study further how to ask and answer questions.

Nasaan ang barangay Katipunan?	Where + **ang** + Barangay Katipunan? *Where + Barangay Katipunan?*
Nasa lungsod ng Quezon ang barangay Katipunan.	In + city + of + Quezon + **ang** + Barangay Katipunan. *Barangay Katipunan is in Quezon City.*
ano	*what*
anong	*what* (contraction of **ano** + **na**)
anong probinsiya	*what province*
nasa anong probinsiya	*in what province*
lungsod ng Calamba	city + of + Calamba. *Calamba City*
Nasa anong probinsiya ang lungsod ng Calamba?	In + what + province + **ang** + city + of + Calamba? *In what province is Calamba City?*
Nasa probinsiya ng Laguna ang lungsod ng Calamba.	In + province + of + Laguna + **ang** + city + of + Calamba. *Calamba City is in the province of Laguna.*
alin	*which*
aling	*which* (contraction of **alin** + **na**)
nasa aling isla	*in which island*
isla ng Luzon	island + of + Luzon. *Luzon island*
Nasa aling isla ang probinsiya ng Laguna?	In + which + island + **ang** + province + of + Laguna. *In which island is the province of Laguna?*
nasa isla ng Luzon	in + island + of + Luzon. *In Luzon island*
probinsiya ng Laguna	province + of + Laguna. *Laguna province*
Ano ang Luzon?	*What is Luzon?*
isa	literally, *one* (used for the English article *a*)
isang	*one* (contraction of **isa** + **na**)
isang isla	*an island* (literally, *one island*)
Isang isla ang Luzon.	An + island + **ang** + Luzon. *Luzon is an island.*
Saan sa...	*Where in ...*
Saan sa Luzon...	*Where in Luzon ...*

Saan sa Luzon ka nakatira?	Where + in + Luzon + you + live? *Where in Luzon do you live?*
Nakatira ako sa lungsod ng Calamba.	Live + I + in + city + of + Calamba. *I live in Calamba City.*

Where is Cabanatuan?

Study the dialogue below. Note the placement of the honorific **po** immediately following the first word in the sentence.

RALPH	:	**Taga-saan po kayo, Mr. Tolentino?** *Where are you from, Mr. Tolentino?*
MR. TOLENTINO	:	**Taga-Cabanatuan ako.** *I am from Cabanatuan.*
RALPH	:	**Nasaan po ang Cabanatuan?** *Where is Cabanatuan?*
MR. TOLENTINO	:	**Nasa Nueva Ecija ang Cabanatuan. Ikaw?** *Cabanatuan is in Nueva Ecija. And you?*
RALPH	:	**Taga-New York po ako.** *I am from New York.*
MR. TOLENTINO	:	**Saan sa New York?** *Where in New York?*
RALPH	:	**Sa Manhattan po.** *(In) Manhattan.*

Practice the dialogue.

QUESTION AND ANSWER PRACTICE

Use the first few questions and answers as a guide. Then practice what you have just learned. For the answers, you may want to refer back to the sentences and dialogues you have learned in this chapter.

1. Question: **Taga-saan ka?** *Where are you from?*

   Answer: **Taga-Santa Barbara ako.** *I am from Santa Barbara.*

2. Question: **Nasaan ang Santa Barbara?** *Where is Santa Barbara?*

   Answer: **Nasa California ang Santa Barbara.** *Santa Barbara is in California.*

3. Question: **Saan ka nakatira?** *Where do you live?*

   Answer: **Nakatira ako sa Barangay San Jose.** *I live in Barangay San Jose.*

4. Question: **Nasa anong lungsod ang Barangay San Jose?**
   In which city is Barangay San Jose?

   Answer: _____.

5. Question: **Taga-saan si Ralph?**

   Answer: _____.

6. Question: _____?

   Answer: **Taga-Cabanatuan City si Mr. Tolentino.**

7. Question: _____?

   Answer: **Nakatira si Mr. Tolentino sa Makati.**

8. Question: **Nasaan ang Manhattan?**

   Answer: _____.

9. Question: _____?

   Answer: **Nasa isla ng Mindanao ang Davao.**

10. Question: _____?

    Answer: **Nasa probinsiya ng Bulacan ang bayan ng Malolos.**

11. Question: **Taga-saan ka?**

    Answer: _____.

12. Question: **Saan ka nakatira ngayon?**

    Answer: _____.

GRAMMAR

In this chapter, we are learning/reviewing the following:

1. The following question words:

ano   *what*
alin   *which*
saan   *where* (used only when there is a verb, for example, **nakatira**)
nasaan *where* (used when there are no verbs)

2. The linker **na**

In general, **na** is used to link words, phrases and clauses. In this chapter, in particular we learned how to use it with question words, and in forming contracted question words.

anong	ano + na
anong lungsod	*what city*
aling (alin + na)	*which*
aling probinsiya	*which province*
saan	*where*
saang (saan + na)	*where*
saang probinsiya	*which place* (literally, where place)

We do not link **na** with **nasaan**. **Nasaan** is usually followed by the marker **ang**.

Nasaan ang lungsod ng Quezon? *Where is Quezon city?*

3. The word **isa** for the English articles *a/an*

There are no articles in Tagalog. Instead, we use the word **isa**, which literally means *one*.

isa	*one* (used as an article)
isang	*one* (contraction of **isa** + **na**)
isang lungsod	one + LINKER + city
Isang lungsod ang Calamba.	One + LINKER + city + **ang** + Calamba. *Calamba is a city.*

4. The words **noon** (*then, previously, in the past*), **ngayon** (*now*) and the affix **naka-**

Review the following sentences:

Nakatira ako sa Manhattan noon.	Live + I + in + Manhattan + previously. *I used to live in Manhattan.*
Nakatira na ako sa Quezon City ngayon.	Live + already + I + in + Quezon City + now. *I now live in Quezon City.*

Note that in English, the first sentence is in the past tense—with the phrase "used to live," while the second sentence is in the present tense with the use of the verb or action word "live." However, in Tagalog, we see that we have the same verb—**nakatira** (*live/living*).

Nakatira is formed by the affix **naka-** and the root word **tira** (live). The affix **naka-** shows a person's state or condition. For example: **nakatayo** (standing), **nakaupo** (sitting), **nakasuot** (wearing).

This brings us to the question: Are there tenses—past, present, and future—in Tagalog?

There are two schools of thought when it comes to Tagalog verbs. Some grammarians, such as Paraluman Aspillera, use tenses (absolute location of an event or action in time) in explaining Tagalog grammar. Other grammarians, such as Paul Schacter and Teresita Ramos, believe that there are aspects (refers how an action is to be viewed in respect to time)—completed action, incompleted action, and contemplated action. It may be better to think of Tagalog verbs in terms of aspects because there is no absolute concept of time in both the Tagalog language and Filipino culture.

There are three ways of saying "I used to live in Manhattan."

1. **Nakatira ako sa Manhattan noon.** Live + I + in + Manhattan + previously.
   (literally, I living in Manhattan previously.)

2. **Tumira ako sa Manhattan noon.** Lived + I + in + Manhattan + previously.
   (literally, I lived in Manhattan previously.)

3. **Tumitira ako sa Manhattan noong nag-aaral ako.** Living + I + in + Manhattan + previously + when + studying. (literally, I was living in Manhattan when I was studying.)

in the first sentence, the affix **naka-** is used to show a state or condition. In the second sentence, the word **tira** is conjugated by inserting the prefix **um-** before the first vowel in order to express completed action. In the third sentence, we can observe that in Tagalog, it is fine to use the incompleted aspect. In this sentence, **tumitira** is translated as *was living*, but the same word can also be used to mean *live/living* (present tense).

We will learn more of verbs in other chapters.

What is your nationality?

Finally, let's study nationality, ethnicity, and names of countries. Study these words, phrases and sentences, then the dialogue.

nasyonalidad	*nationality*
ano ang	*what is*
Ano ang nasyonalidad mo?	What + **ang** + nationality + your? *What is your nationality?*

etnisidad	*ethnicity*
Filipino	*Filipino*
Filipino ang etnisidad ko	Filipino + **ang** + ethnicity + my.
	My ethnicity is Filipino.
Filipino American ako.	Filipino American + I
	I am Filipino American.
mamamayan	*citizen*
Estados Unidos	*United States*
mamamayan ng Estados Unidos	*citizen of the United States.*
Mamamayan ako ng Estados Unidos.	Citizen + I + of + United States.
	I am a citizen of the United States.
Amerikano	*American*
Amerikano ako	American + I. *I am American.*
pero	*but*
Amerikano ako pero Filipino ang etnisidad ko.	American + I + but + Filipino + **ang** + ethnicity + my.
	I am American but my ethnicity is Filipino.

Note: If one wanted to say, for example, "*I'm a citizen of the United States,*" one could probably say "**Mamamayan ako ng Estados Unidos.**" However, in colloquial Tagalog, one would probably say, "**Amerikano ako.**" (*I am an American citizen.*)

 **DIALOGUE C**

Read the following dialogue between Ralph and Melissa.

RALPH : **Ano ang nasyonalidad mo, Melissa?** *What is your nationality, Melissa?*

MELISSA : **Amerikano ako. Pero Filipino ang etnisidad ko. Ikaw?** *I am American. But my ethnicity is Filipino. And you?*

RALPH : **Amerikano ako pero Italyano ang etnisidad ko.** *I am American, but my ethnicity is Italian.*

VOCABULARY

Here are other nationalities and names of countries in Tagalog. Some of these words are borrowed from other languages, such as English or Spanish.

English	Tagalog	
	Country	People
United States	Estados Unidos	Amerikano
Japan	Hapon	Hapon (m)/Haponesa (f)
China	Tsina	Tsino (m)/Tsina (f)
Great Britain	Inglatera	Briton
Russia	Rusya	Ruso
Spain	Espanya	Kastila

m = male; f = female

Now, try to answer the following questions:

1. Question: **Ano ang etnisidad mo?**

   Answer: _____.

2. Question: **Ano ang nasyonalidad mo?**

   Answer: _____.

SUMMING UP

Let us review what you have just learned in Chapter 2.

Fill in the blanks for the first two paragraphs about Ralph and Melissa. Then, using the cues in these two paragraphs, write a sentence about yourself.

Taga-_____ si Melissa. Amerikano _____. Nakatira siya

ngayon sa _____. _____ ang etnisidad niya.

Taga-_____ si Ralph. _____ siya.

_____ ngayon sa Makati. _____ ang etnisidad

_____.

CHAPTER 3

What is your job?
Ano ang trabaho mo?

Sarah is an advertising account executive at Orendain Advertising; Mr. Tolentino is a lawyer; and Melissa is a student. In this dialogue, learn how to talk about jobs and professions. Study how the two question words you have learned, **ano** (*what*) and **saan** (*where*), are used, and how sentences are constructed to ask and answer these questions.

Jobs and Professions

estudyante	*student*
account executive	*account executive*
abugado	*lawyer*
Abugado ako.	Lawyer + I. *I am a lawyer.* (informal)
Abugado po ako.	*I am a lawyer.* (formal)
Ano ang trabaho mo?	What + **ang** + job + your? *What is your job?*
Account executive po ako.	*I am an account executive.* (formal)
namumuno	*to head* or *to be in charge of*
ako ang namumuno	I + **ang** + *head*
Ako ang namumuno sa Legal Department.	I + **ang** + head + in + Legal Department. *I head the Legal Department.*
pinuno	*head*
ako ang pinuno	I + **ang** + head. *I am the head*
Ako ang pinuno ng Legal Department.	I + **ang** + head + of + Legal Department. *I am the head of the Legal Department.*
saan	*where*
nagtatrabaho	*work*
Saan po kayo nagtatrabaho?	Where + you + work? *Where do you work?* (formal)

Nagtatrabaho ako sa North American Investment Bank.	Work + I + at + North American Investment Bank. *I work at North American Investment Bank.*
nag-aaral	*study*
Saan ka nag-aaral?	Where + you + study? *Where do you study?*
Nag-aaral ako sa Unibersidad ng Pilipinas.	Study + I + at + University + of + Philippines. *I study at the University of the Philippines.*
namin	*our* (1st person plural possessive pronoun; refers only to the speaker and his/her companions)
natin	*our* (1st person plural possessive pronoun; refers to the speakers and the people being addressed; literally, we + you)
kliyente namin	*our client*
ninyo	*your* (2nd person plural possessive pronoun)
bangko ninyo	*your bank*
Kliyente po namin ang bangko ninyo.	Client + po + our + **ang** + bank + your. *Your bank is our client.*
nila	*their* (3rd person plural possessive pronoun)
bangko nila	*their bank*
Kliyente po namin ang bangko nila.	Client + po + our + **ang** + bank + their. *Their bank is our client.*

DIALOGUE A

SARAH : **Saan po kayo nagtatrabaho, Mr. Tolentino?** *Where do you work, Mr. Tolentino?*

MR. TOLENTINO : **Sa North American Investment Bank. Ako ang namumuno sa Legal Department. Ikaw, ano ang trabaho mo?** *At the North American Investment Bank. I head the Legal Department. What about you, what is your job?*

SARAH : **Advertising account executive po ako. Kliyente po namin ang bangko ninyo.** *I am an advertising account executive. Your bank is our client.*

MR. TOLENTINO : **Ganoon ba? Saan ka nagtatrabaho?** *Is that so? Where do you work?*

SARAH : **Sa Orendain Advertising po.** *At Orendain Advertising.*

MR. TOLENTINO : **Talaga? Ikaw, Melissa?** *Really? What about you, Melissa?*

MELISSA : **Estudyante po ako. Nag-aaral ako sa Unibersidad ng Pilipinas.** *I am a student. I study at the University of the Philippines.*

VOCABULARY AND SENTENCE PRACTICE

For some professions, Tagalog uses loanwords from other languages. Examples of these are: social worker, computer programmer, and website designer. In some cases, the words are derived from English but have a Tagalog spelling. Here are other words you can use.

manedyer ng bangko	*bank manager*
guro/titser	*teacher*
doktor	*doctor*
nars	*nurse*
kawani	*employee*
kawani ng gobyerno	*government employee*
abugado	*lawyer*
inhinyero	*engineer*
arkitekto	*architect*
mananaliksik	*researcher*
manggagawa	*worker*
drayber	*driver*
magsasaka	*farmer*
negosyante	*businessperson*
manunulat	*writer*
bumbero	*fireman*
pulis	*police officer*

For natural speech, study the following expressions:

Talaga?	*Really?*
Ganoon ba?	*Is that so?*

Also, review the following linkers and markers.

na (sometimes contracted into **ng**) linker (used to link words)

ng preposition; object marker (used to introduce the object of a sentence; used for common nouns)

si subject marker (used to introduce the subject of a sentence; used for names or proper nouns)

ni possessive and object marker (used to introduce proper nouns)

Notice the phrase **manedyer ng bangko** (*bank manager*) above. **Ng** is a preposition. It can mean *in*, *on*, *of*, and *at*. In the example below, it is used to mean "of." Note that pronouns go immediately after **manedyer** (manager) and before the preposition. Study the following phrases and sentences:

manedyer ng bangko	manager + of + bank. *bank manager*
Manedyer ng bangko si Ralph.	Manager + of + bank + **si** + Ralph. *Ralph is a bank manager.*
Manedyer ka ng bangko.	Manager + you + of + bank. *You are a bank manager.*
Estudyante si Melissa.	Student + **si** + Melissa. *Melissa is a student.*
Account executive si Sarah sa Orendain Advertising.	Account executive + **si** + Sarah + at + Orendain Advertising. *Sarah is an account executive at Orendain Advertising.*
Doktor ako.	Doctor + I. *I am a doctor.*

QUESTION AND ANSWER PRACTICE

Practice asking and answering questions. The first pairs are there to serve as your guide. If your job/profession was not listed earlier, just use the English word for now. The important thing is to study the structure of the sentence. Remember that we are practicing the question words **ano** (*what*) and **saan** (*where*).

1. Question: **Ano ang trabaho mo?**
   Answer: **Guro ako.**

2. Question: **Ano ang trabaho ni Mr. Tolentino?**
   Answer: **Abugado siya.**

3. Question: **Ano ang trabaho ni Melissa?**
   Answer: _____.

4. Question: _____?
   Answer: **Nars siya.**

5. Question: **Ano ang** _____?
   Answer: **Kawani siya ng bangko.**

6. Question: **Ano ang trabaho mo?**

   Answer: _____.

GRAMMAR: VERBS

In Tagalog, it is important to know root words. With root words, we can use affixes to form verbs, nouns, adjectives, and adverbs. In this chapter we are focusing on root words and the prefix **mag-** (with its variation **nag-**) for verbs.

In these examples, study how the verbs **nag-aaral** (*study*) and **nagtatrabaho** (*work*) are formed and used.

aral	*study* (root word)
nag-	verb prefix
nag- + a + aral	**nag** + first syllable of root word + root word; *study*
nag-aaral ako	*I study*
Nag-aaral ako sa UCLA.	Study + I + at + UCLA. *I study at UCLA.*
trabaho	*work*
nag + ta + trabaho	**nag** + first syllable of root word + root word (Rule: when the word has double consonants such as **tr** in **trabaho**, **r** is dropped in the second syllable); *work*
Nagtatrabaho ako sa Filipino Community Center.	Work + I + at + Filipino Community Center. *I work at the Filipino Community Center.*

Let us also study three special verbs: **naging** (*became*), **nag-master's** (*studied for a master's degree*) and **nag-training** (*trained*). **Naging** (*became*) is referred to as an independent verb because it is not formed by a prefix and a root word. **Nag-master's** (*studied for a master's degree*) and **nag-training** (*trained*) are also special because the two words are formed by using the Tagalog prefix **nag-** and the English words, *master's* and *train*, respectively.

naging abugado	became + lawyer.
Naging abugado ako.	Became + lawyer + I. *I became a lawyer.*
Nagma-master's ako.	Taking a master's degree + I. *I am taking a master's degree.*

In the previous chapter, we learned about verb aspects in Tagalog. Completed action can be thought of as the past tense in English, incompleted action as the present tense, and contemplated action as the future tense. The main differences between aspects (completed, incompleted, contemplated) and tenses (past, present, future) lie mainly in the perfect tenses (for example, *has/have been, had worked*) and the progressive tenses (for example, *has/have been working*). If it is easier for you to think of verbs using the terms simple past, present, and future tenses, use these terms instead.

There are specific formulas to conjugate verbs in Tagalog. Study the following formulas and how these are used with the root word **aral** (*study*).

Completed   prefix **nag-** + root word
(Past) Action   **nag + aral = nag-aral**

Incompleted   prefix **nag-** + first syllable of root word + root word
(Present) Action   **nag- + a + ara**l = **nag-aaral**

Contemplated   prefix **mag-** + first syllable of root word + root word
(Future) Action   **mag- + a + aral = mag-aaral**

Study the following chart:

Root	Completed	Incompleted	Contemplated
aral *study*	**nag-aral** *studied*	**nag-aaral** *studying*	**mag-aaral** *will study*
trabaho *work*	**nagtrabaho** *worked*	**nagtatrabaho** *working*	**magtatrabaho** *will work*
maging *to become*	**naging** *become*	**nagiging** *becoming*	**magiging** *will become*
masters *to take a master's degree* (used as a verb)	**nag-masters** *took a master's degree*	**nagma-masters** *taking a master's degree*	**magma-masters** *will take a master's degree*
training *to train* (used as a verb)	**nag-training** *trained*	**nagte-training** *training*	**magte-training** *will train*

Note that when we duplicate the first syllable in words with double consonants, for example, **tr** in **nagtatrabaho** (**nag** + **ta** + **trabaho**), we omit the second consonant (**ta** and not **tra**). However, bear in mind that this is only important in written Tagalog. In colloquial speech, we can say either **nagtratrabaho** or **nagtatrabaho**.

Studying and Working

Study how the verbs you have learned are used in the following dialogue.

Mr. Tolentino	:	**Saan ka nag-aral, Ralph?** *Where did you study, Ralph?*
Ralph	:	**Sa UCLA po. Kayo po?** *At UCLA. What about you?*
Mr. Tolentino	:	**Sa UP, pero nag-master's ako ng abugasya sa Netherlands.** *At U.P., but I took my master's in law in the Netherlands.*
Sarah	:	**Talaga po? Mag-aaral din ako sa Netherlands next year.** *Really? I will also study in the Netherlands next year.*
Ralph	:	**Saan ka magtatrabaho after graduation, Melissa?** *Where will you work after graduation, Melissa?*
Melissa	:	**Magtatrabaho po ako sa Center for Community Health. Magiging community health worker po ako.** *I will work for the Center for Community Health. I will become a community health worker.*

> **VOCABULARY AND CULTURE TIP (Taglish)** Taglish refers to Tagalog-English, the colloquial way of speaking wherein people, especially those living in urban centers, use both Tagalog/Filipino and English in a sentence. Thus, Sarah's line **"Mag-aaral din ako sa Netherlands next year"** is not unusual. If in a similar situation you are at a loss for Tagalog words, you can say, for example, **"Nag-work po ako sa hospital for two years."** No one will fault you if five out of eight of the words you use are in English.

QUESTION AND ANSWER PRACTICE

Ask and answer the following questions:

1. Question: **Saan nagtatrabaho si Ralph?**

   Answer: _____ **si Ralph sa** _____.

2. Question: **Saan nag-aaral si Melissa?**

   Answer: _____

3. Question: **Saan nag-aral si Mr. Tolentino?**

   Answer: _____ **si** _____ **sa** _____.

4. Question: **Saan ka nagtatrabaho?**

   Answer: _____.

5. Question: **Saan ka nag-aral?**

   Answer: _____.

6. Question: _____?

   Answer: **Nag-aral si Sarah sa Unibersidad ng Pilipinas.**

SENTENCE STRUCTURE AND GRAMMAR

Let us practice the verbs we have learned, using **saan** (*where*) and a new question word, **kailan** (*when*).

Study the following questions and answers.

Saan ka nagtrabaho?	Where + you + worked? *Where did you work?*
Nagtrabaho ako sa Philippine Bank.	Worked + I + at + Philippine Bank. *I worked at Philippine Bank.*
Saan ka nagtatrabaho?	Where + you + work? *Where do you work?*
Nagtatrabaho ako sa Singapore Bank.	Work + I + at + Singapore Bank. *I work at Singapore Bank.*
Saan ka magtatrabaho?	Where + you + will work? *Where will you work?*
Magtatrabaho ako sa National Bank.	Will work + I + at + National Bank. *I will work at National Bank.*
Ano ang trabaho mo?	What + **ang** + work + your + job? *What is/was your job?*

Accountant ako.	Accountant + I. *I am/was an accountant.*
kailan	*when*
kailan ka nagtrabaho	when + you + worked
Kailan ka nagtrabaho sa Philippine Bank?	When + you + worked + at Philippine Bank? *When did you work at Philippine Bank?*
noon [no'on]	*in the past* (also used to mean *in, on*)
noong	*in the past* (contraction of **noon** + **na**)
noong 2012	*in 2012*
Nagtrabaho ako sa Philippine Bank noong 2012.	*I worked at Philippine Bank in 2012.*
ngayon	*now; at present*
Nagtatrabaho ako sa Singapore ngayon.	Work + I + Singapore Bank + now. *I work at Singapore Bank now.*
Naging abugado ako noong 2008.	Became + lawyer + I + in 2008. *I became a lawyer in 2008.*
Nag-master's ako noong 2012.	Took a master's degree + I + in + 2010. *I took a master's degree in 2010.*
mula	*from*
hanggang	*to*
mula 2010 hanggang 2012	*from 2010 to 2012*

Nag-master's ako mula 2010 hanggang 2012.	Took a master's degree + I + from 2010 to 2012. *I took a master's degree from 2010 to 2012.*

Here are some useful grammar points:

1. **Flexibility.** Usually, there is more than one way of saying or asking the same thing. For example, If we want to ask someone what his job was in the past, we can say, "**Ano ang trabaho mo?**" (*What is/was your job?*) or "**Ano ang trabaho mo noon?**" (*What was your job then?*)

2. **The Verb "to be."** There is no exact equivalent for the English verb "to be" (*am, is, are*) in Tagalog. Simply say "**Accountant ako.**" (literally, *Accountant I*).

3. **Aspects and Tenses.** Grammar point number 2 gives us a better understanding as to why some grammarians insist that there are no tenses (past, present, future) in Tagalog, and just aspects (completed action, incompleted action, and contemplated action). "I was an accountant" and "I am an accountant" can both be translated as "**Accountant ako.**"

4. **Prepositions:** The Tagalog words **noon/noong** (*then;* used to mean *in*) and **sa** (*in, at*) both mean the English preposition *in*. However, **noon/noong** is used only when the action has been completed. Here are some examples:

Nagtrabaho ako sa Philippine Bank noong 2012.	Work + I + at + Philippine Bank in 2012. *I worked at the Philippine Bank in 2012.*
Magtatrabaho ako sa National Bank next year.	Will + work + I + National Bank + next year. *I will work at the National Bank next year.*

Remember to use **noon** as a preposition for past action, and **sa** for future action.

QUESTION AND ANSWER PRACTICE

1. Question: **Saan ka nagtrabaho noon?**

   Answer: _____ ako sa _____.

2. Question: **Saan magtatrabaho si Melissa?**

   Answer: _____ si Melissa sa _____.

3. Question: **Kailan ka magtatrabaho sa _____?**

   Answer: _____.

4. **Kailan ka nag-aral sa _____?**

   Answer: _____.

SUMMING UP

Let us review what you have just learned in Chapter 3.

Talk about your studies and work in the past, present and future.

_____

_____

_____

_____

_____

_____

_____

_____

_____

_____

CHAPTER 4

What is your mother's name?
Ano ang pangalan ng nanay mo?

In this chapter, we will learn about family members and we will learn some adjectives.

Family Relations

Melissa and Mr. Tolentino discover that they are distantly related because Melissa's aunt, Luna Sicat, is Mr. Tolentino's second cousin.

Review/study the following words, phrases, and sentences used in the dialogue:

nanay	*mother*
tatay	*father*
pamilya	*family*
taga-saan	*from where*
Taga-saan ang nanay mo?	From-where + **ang** + mother + your? *Where is your mother from?*
Taga-Cabanatuan ang nanay ko.	From-Cabanatuan + **ang** + mother + my. *My mother is from Cabanatuan.*
pamilya ng tatay ko	family + of + father + my. *my father's family*
din	*also*
Taga-Cabanatuan din ang pamilya ng tatay ko.	From-Cabanatuan + also + **ang** family + of + father + my. *My father's family is also from Cabanatuan.*
apelyido	*last name, family name*
Ano ang apelyido ng nanay mo?	What + **ang** + last name + of + mother + your? *What is your mother's last name?*
kaano-ano	*how are you related to* (literally, *how related*)
Kaano-ano mo si Luna Sicat?	How related + you + **si** + Luna Sicat? *How are you related to Luna Sicat?*

tiya	*aunt*
Tiya ko siya.	Aunt + my + she. *She is my aunt.* (informal)
Tiya ko po siya.	*She is my aunt.* (formal)
pinsan	*cousin*
Pinsan ko siya.	Cousin + my + she. *She is my cousin.*
kapatid	*sibling, brother/sister*
Kapatid ko siya.	Sibling + my + he/she. *He/she is my sibling.*
magkapatid	*siblings*
kami	*we*
Magkapatid kami.	Siblings + we. *We are siblings.*
lola	*grandmother*
lolo	*grandfather*
mga	word used to make a noun plural
mga lola	*grandmothers*
mga lolo	*grandfathers*
Magkapatid ang	Siblings + **ang** + grandmothers + our.
mga lola namin.	*Our grandmothers are siblings.*
tiyo	*uncle*
pala	expression used when something is unexpected (used like *Oh!*)
Tiyo ko kayo.	Uncle + my + you. *You are my uncle.*
Tiyo ko pala kayo!	Uncle + my + oh + you! *Oh, so you are my uncle!*
kaya	*because* (literally, *that's why*)
maganda	*beautiful*
Maganda ka.	Beautiful + you. *You are beautiful.*
Kaya pala	That's why + oh + beautiful + you.
maganda ka.	*So that's why you're beautiful.*

◉ DIALOGUE A

MR. TOLENTINO : **Taga-saan ang nanay mo, Melissa?** *Where is your mother from, Melissa?*

MELISSA : **Taga-Cabanatuan po.** *From Cabanatuan.*

Mr. Tolentino	:	Talaga? Taga-Cabanatuan din ang pamilya ng tatay ko. Ano ba ang apelyido ng nanay mo? *Really? My father's family is also from Cabanatuan. What is your mother's family name?*
Melissa	:	Sicat po. *Sicat.*
Mr. Tolentino	:	Kaano-ano mo si Luna Sicat? *(How) are you related to Luna Sicat?*
Melissa	:	Tiya ko po siya. *She is my aunt.*
Mr. Tolentino	:	Pinsan ko siya. Magkapatid ang mga lola namin. *She is my cousin. Our grandmothers are sisters.*
Melissa	:	Tiyo ko pala kayo! *You are my uncle!*
Mr. Tolentino	:	Kaya pala maganda ka. *So that's why you are beautiful.*

VOCABULARY AND SENTENCE STRUCTURE

Here are additional words you can use when talking about your family. Also review how to pluralize nouns using the word **mga**, which you learned in Chapter 1.

nanay/inay/ina	*mother*
tatay/itay/ama	*father*
magulang	*parent*
mga magulang	*parents*
anak	*child*
mga anak	*children*
kapatid	*brother/sister*
ate	*elder sister*
kuya	*elder brother*
lolo	*grandfather*
lola	*grandmother*
apo	*grandchild*
tiyo/tiyuhin/tito	*uncle*
tiya/tiyahin/tita	*aunt*
manugang na babae	*daughter-in-law*
manugang na lalaki	*son-in-law*
bayaw	*brother-in-law*
bilas	*sister-in law*
pamangkin	*niece/nephew*
alagang pusa	*pet cat*

alagang aso	*pet dog*
alagang hayop	*pet*
sino	*who*
Sino siya?	Who + he/she? *Who is he/she?*
Kapatid ko siya.	Sibling + my + he/she. *He/she is my brother/sister.*
ito	*this*
Sino ito?	Who + this? *Who is this?*
Alagang pusa ko ito.	Pet cat + my + this. *This is my pet cat.*

To talk about the gender and age, you can use the following words, phrases and sentences.

babae	*woman/female*
lalaki	*man/male*
bakla	*gay*
lesbiana	*lesbian*
transgender	*transgender*
Babae ang anak ko.	Female + **ang** + child + my. *My child is female.*
bata	*young* (adjective) (this can also mean *child*)
matanda	*old*
pa	*still* or *yet* (in this chapter)
bata pa	*still young*
mga anak	*children*
Bata pa ang mga anak ko.	Young + still + **ang** + children + my. *My children are still young.*
na	*already* (in this chapter)
matanda na	*already old*
Matanda na ang mga magulang ko.	Old + already + **ang** + parents + my. *My parents are already old.*
nasa	*at, in,* or *on* (in this chapter)
sapat	*sufficient*
gulang	*age*
nasa sapat na gulang	*adult* (literally, *at sufficient age*)
nasa sapat na gulang na	*already an adult* (literally, *adult already*)

Nasa wastong gulang na ako.	Adult + already + I. *I am an adult.*
bata	*child* (in this chapter)
Bata siya.	Child + he/she. *He/she is a child.*

Here are some adjectives, phrases, and sentences that you can use when talking about your family members:

maganda	*beautiful; pretty* (used for women)
guwapo/makisig	*handsome* (used for men)
mabait	*good*
masungit	*grouchy*
matalino	*intelligent*
matulungin	*helpful*
mahiyain	*shy*
masipag	*hard-working*
mayaman	*rich*
mahirap	*poor*
madaldal	*talkative*
matangkad	*tall* (used for people)
palakaibigan	*friendly*

Matangkad ang nanay ko.	Tall + **ang** + mother + my. *My mother is tall.*
Matulungin ang tatay ko.	Helpful + **ang** + father + my. *My father is helpful.*

SENTENCE PRACTICE

Study the following sentence patterns, and then try to fill in the blanks.

Ako si Melissa. Cynthia ang pangalan ng nanay ko. Matalino siya.

Siya si Sarah. Arnold ang pangalan ng kapatid niya. Mabait si Arnold.

Ako si _____. _____ ang pangalan ng _____

ko. _____ siya.

Now, try to write more sentences describing the members of your family.

_____

_____

VOCABULARY AND CULTURE TIP (Familiarity) When you go shopping in the Philippines, some vendors or salespeople may call you **ate** (*elder sister*) or **kuya** (*elder brother*). Meanwhile, some news reporters call their audiences **kapamilya** (*of the same family*). Filipinos try to build personal connections by using words that refer to family members. Don't be offended if someone calls you Elder Brother or Elder Sister!

VOCABULARY AND SENTENCE STRUCTURE

Review the adjectives you learned earlier in this chapter, and see how comparatives are used:

mas	*more*
bata	*young*
mas bata	*younger* (literally, *more young*)
mas bata siya	younger + he/she. *he/she is younger*
akin	*I, me,* or *my*
sa	preposition used to mean *in, on,* or *at*
kaysa	*than*
kaysa sa akin	*than me*
Mas bata siya kaysa sa akin.	Younger + he/she + than + me. *He/she is younger than me.*
mas matangkad	*taller*
Mas matangkad siya kaysa sa akin.	Taller + he/she + than + I. *He/she is taller than me.*
pero	*but*
Mas bata siya kaysa sa akin pero mas matangkad.	Younger + he/she + than + me + but + taller. *He/she is younger than me but taller.*
pinaka-	prefix, *most*
pinakamatangkad	*tallest* (literally, *most tall*)
Pinakamatangkad ang tatay ko.	Tallest + **ang** + father + my. *My father is the tallest.*
pinakamaganda	*most beautiful*
sa pamilya	*in the family*
Pinakamaganda ang nanay ko sa pamilya.	Most beautiful + **ang** + mother + my + in + family. *My mother is the most beautiful in the family.*

GRAMMAR

Comparatives and Superlatives

For comparatives, we use the words **mas** (*more*) before the adjective and **kaysa** (*than*) between the two people/objects being compared. In the sentence patterns below, note the use of the object marker **kay** (used when comparing people), and the preposition **sa** (used after **kaysa** with pronouns or when comparing objects). **Kaysa** can be omitted in conversational Tagalog.

kay	object marker used before names or proper nouns
kaysa kay Sarah	*than Sarah*
sa	preposition used to mean *in, an, on*, etc.
kaysa sa kaibigan ko	*than my friend*
kaysa sa iyo	*than you*

Ralph is taller than Sarah.
Mas matangkad si Ralph kaysa kay Sarah.
Mas matangkad si Ralph kay Sarah.

I am taller than you.
Mas matangkad ako kaysa sa iyo.
Mas matangkad ako sa iyo.

For superlatives, attach the affix **pinaka-** to the adjective. Note that you can change the word order. However, pronouns must come immediately after the adjective.

My elder sister is the most hard-working in the family.
Pinakamasipag ang ate ko sa pamilya.
Pinakamasipag sa pamilya ang ate ko.

I am the youngest in the family.
Pinakabata ako sa pamilya ko.

Family Picture

Ralph is showing Sarah a picture of his family.

SARAH : **Sino ito?** *Who is this?*

RALPH : **Kapatid ko ito. Mas bata siya sa akin pero mas matangkad.**
This is my brother. He is younger but he is taller.

SARAH : **Sino ang pinakamatangkad?** *Who is the tallest?*

RALPH : **Ang tatay ko.** *My father.*

SARAH : **Sino ang pinakamaganda?** *Who is the prettiest?*

RALPH : **Pinakamaganda ang nanay ko sa pamilya.** *My mother is the prettiest.*

GRAMMAR
Pronouns

Let us review/study pronouns using this chart.

Personal pronouns chart

Subject pronouns	Object pronouns	Possessive adjectives	Possessive pronouns
ako *I*	akin *me*	ko, akin *my*	akin *mine*
ikaw, ka *you*	iyo *you*	mo, iyo *your*	iyo *yours*
siya *he/she*	kanya *her/him*	niya, kanya *his/her*	kanya *his/hers*
kami (exclusive) *we* tayo (inclusive) *we* (means *we + you*)	amin (exclusive) *us* atin (inclusive) *us* (means *us + you*)	amin, namin (inclusive) *our* atin, natin (exclusive) *our* (means *our + your*)	amin (inclusive) *ours* atin (exclusive) *ours* (means *ours + yours*)
kayo *you* (plural)	inyo *you* (plural)	inyo, ninyo *your* (plural)	ninyo *yours* (plural)
sila *they*	kanila *them*	nila, kanila *their*	kanila *theirs*

Notes:

1. Sometimes two pronouns can be used to mean the same thing. An example is **ko** and **akin**, both of which mean *my*. However, in the case of **akin**, you need the linker **na**, to link it to the noun or subject.

nanay ko   *my mother* (literally, *mother my*)

Siya ang nanay ko.	She + **ang** + mother + my. *She is my mother.*
aking (contraction of **akin** + **na**)	*my*
aking nanay	*my mother*
Siya ang aking nanay.	She + **ang** + my + mother. *She is my mother.*

2. A characteristic of the Tagalog language that is difficult for learners to grasp is the flexibility of meaning. Among the pronouns, for example, **akin** can mean *me*, *my*, and *mine*.

Mas matangkad siya kaysa sa akin.	Taller + he/she + than + me. *He/she is taller than me.*
Matangkad ang aking tatay.	Tall + **ang** + my + father. *My father is tall.*
Akin ito.	Mine + this. *This is mine.*

QUESTION AND ANSWER PRACTICE

Answer these questions and talk about your family. Or, use your imagination and talk about a fictitious family.

1. Question: **Sino ang pinakamatangkad sa pamilya mo?**

    Answer: **Pinakamatangkad si _____ sa pamilya ko.**

2. Question: **Sino ang mas bata, si _____ o si _____?**

    Answer: _____.

3. Question: **Sino ang pinakamabait?**

    Answer: _____.

4. Question: _____?

    Answer: **Mas matalino si _____ kaysa kay _____.**

5. Question: _____?

    Answer: **Mas masungit ang pusa ko kaysa sa aso ko.**

SUMMING UP

Let us try to sum up what you have learned in Chapter 4.

Talk or write a few sentences about your family. Use adjectives, including comparatives and superlatives.

CHAPTER 5

Where is our cat, Muning?
Nasaan si Muning, ang ating pusa?

In this chapter, you will learn about the rooms of a house and practice the use of **nasaan** (*where*).

Looking for Muning

Sarah and Melissa share a two-bedroom apartment. They have a cat, Muning. Sarah is looking for Muning but she cannot find her because the cat is under a table.

Study the following words, phrases, and sentences.

nakita	*saw* or *have seen*
ba	particle for Yes/No questions
nakita mo ba	saw + you + **ba** *have you seen*
Nakita mo ba si Muning?	Saw + you + **ba** + **si** + Muning? *Have you seen Muning?*
oo [pronounced /ó o/]	*yes*
hindi	*no*
nasa	*in* (preposition; can also mean *on* or *at*)
komedor	*dining room*
Nasa komedor siya.	In + dining room + she. *She is in the dining room.*
Nasaan siya?	Where + she? *Where is she?*
nasa ilalim	*under*
mesa	*table*
ng	object marker (used to introduce a noun)
Nasa ilalim siya ng mesa.	Under + she + **ng** + table. *She is under the table.*

MELISSA : **Nakita mo ba si Muning?** *Have you seen Muning?*
SARAH　: **Oo. Nasa komedor siya.** *Yes. She is in the dining room.*
MELISSA : **Nasaan siya?** *Where is she?*
SARAH　: **Nasa ilalim siya ng mesa.** *She is under the table.*

VOCABULARY

Study the words for furniture and rooms of a house.

bahay	*house*
sala	*living room*
komedor/silid-kainan	*dining room*
kuwarto	*bedroom/room*
kusina	*kitchen*
banyo	*bathroom*
hardin	*garden*
garahe	*garage*
mesa	*table*
silya	*chair*
kama	*bed*
sofa	*sofa*

GRAMMAR

Study the following sentences that talk about members of the family and where they are in the house.

Nasa kusina ang tatay ko.	*My father is in the kitchen.*
Nasa garahe ang kuya ko.	*My elder brother is in the garage.*
Nasa hardin ang alagang aso ko.	*My pet dog is in the garden.*

You can practice asking questions to the answers above:

Nasaan ang [insert noun, for example, **tatay**] **mo?**	*Where is your father?*
Nasaan si [insert proper noun, for example, **Muning**]?	*Where is Muning?*

QUESTION AND ANSWER PRACTICE

Now, use the following cues to ask and answer questions. Refer to the vocabulary words above. When asked a **nasaan** (*where*) question, you should start your answer with the word **nasa**.

mother – bedroom
elder sister – bathroom
grandfather – living room
cat – kitchen
aunt – dining room

1. Question: **Nasaan ang nanay mo?**

   Answer: **Nasa** _____ **ang** _____ **ko.**

2. Question: _____ **ang ate mo?**

   Answer: _____ **ang** _____ **ko.**

3. Question: **Nasaan ang lolo mo?**

   Answer: _____.

4. Question: _____?

   Answer: **Nasa kusina ang pusa ko.**

5. Question: _____?

   Answer: _____.

> **VOCABULARY AND CULTURE TIP (Loanwords)** Many Tagalog words were influenced by Spanish words because of 300 years of Spanish colonial rule (1560–1898). If you have a knowledge of Spanish, you will see that many of the words in the vocabulary lists were derived from Spanish.

Around the House

In the earlier dialogue, you studied **nasa ilalim** (*under*). Now, let us practice the use of other prepositions in the following dialogue.

 DIALOGUE B

MELISSA : **Nasaan ang cat food?** *Where is the cat food?*

SARAH : **Nasa loob ng cabinet ng kusina ang cat food. Nakita mo ba ang libro ko?** *The cat food is inside the kitchen cabinet. Have you seen my book?*

Melissa : **Nasa kuwarto ko ang libro mo. Nasa loob ng bag ko.** *Your book is in my room. It is in(side) my bag.*

VOCABULARY

Study the following words that indicate location:

nasa loob   *inside/In*
nasa labas   *outside*
nasa ibabaw   *on top of*
nasa itaas   *above/top part*
nasa ilalim   *under*
nasa ibaba   *below/lower part*

In English, we use prepositions such as *in*, *at*, and *on*. In Tagalog, we simply pair **nasa** with other words to indicate location. See how the words above are used in the following sentences:

Nasa loob ng bag ko ang libro.   *My book is in/inside my bag.*

Nasa loob ng bahay ang nanay ko.   *My mother is inside the house.*

Nasa labas ng bahay ang aso.   *The dog is outside the house.*

Nasa ibabaw ng mesa ang lapis.   *The pencil is on top of/on the table.*

Nasa ilalim ng silya ang pusa.   *The cat is under the chair.*

Nasa itaas ng bahay ang attic.   *The attic is at the top part the house.*

Nasa ibaba ng bahay ang basement.   *The basement is below/at the lower part of the house.*

QUESTION AND ANSWER PRACTICE

Ask and answer questions using the cues given below.

grandmother – inside bathroom
cat – on the bed
punchbowl – above the refrigerator
cereal – inside the kitchen cabinet
nook – under the table

TV antenna – above/top part the house
laundry area – below/lower part of the house

1. Question: **Nasaan ang lola mo?**

   Answer: **Nasa loob ng banyo ang lola ko.**

2. Question: **Nasaan ang pusa?**

   Answer: **Nasa** _____ **ng** _____ **ang pusa.**

3. Question: **Nasaan ang** _____?

   Answer: _____.

4. Question: _____?

   Answer: _____.

5. Question: _____?

   Answer: _____.

6. Question: _____?

   Answer: _____.

Playing with Muning

Melissa is looking for Sarah and their cat, Muning.

Study the following sentences using demonstrative pronouns and adjectives (*here, there*) in Tagalog.

narito	*here*
Narito ako	Here + I. *I am here.*
Narito ako sa sala.	Here + I + in + living room.
	I am here in the living room.
Narito siya.	*She/he is here.*
dito/rito	*here*
naglalaro	playing
Dito kami naglalaro.	Here + we + playing. *We are playing here.*

 DIALOGUE C

MELISSA : **Nasaan ka, Sarah?** *Where are you, Sarah?*

SARAH : **Narito ako sa sala, Melissa.** *I am here in the living room, Melissa.*

MELISSA : **Nasaan si Muning?** *Where is Muning?*

SARAH : **Narito siya. Dito kami naglalaro.** *She is here. We are playing here.*

VOCABULARY AND GRAMMAR

Let us study the equivalents of demonstrative pronouns that indicate location—*here, there,* and *over there.*

dito/rito/nandito/narito	*here*
diyan/riyan/nandiyan/nariyan	*there*
doon/roon/nandoon/naroon	*over there*

Dito and **rito** have exactly the same meaning and are interchangeable in spoken Tagalog. In the indigenous writing system, **baybayin,** the /d/ and /r/ sounds shared the same symbol and were interchangeable. Thus, **diyan** and **riyan, doon** and **roon, nandito** and **narito, nandiyan** and **nariyan** and **nandoon** and **naroon** are interchangeable in spoken Tagalog.

In written Tagalog, we use **dito, diyan,** and **doon** when the preceding word ends with a consonant; and **rito, riyan,** and **roon** when the preceding word ends with a vowel. For example, in the sentences below, **dito** is used after "Muning," while **rito** is used after **ka.**

Naglalaro si Muning dito.	*Muning is playing here.*
Naglalaro ka rito.	*You are playing here.*

In addition, the latest spelling and editing guidelines for written Tagalog published by the University of the Philippines Center for the Filipino Language (2008) specify that because the affix **na-** ends with a vowel, in contracted forms we should use **rito** and **roon,** and not **dito** and **doon.**

na + dito = narito
na + doon = naroon

Study the following sentences.

Narito ako.	*I am here.*
Nariyan si Muning sa kusina.	*Muning is there in the kitchen.*
Naroon ang bag ko sa kuwarto.	*My bag is there in the room.*

As you can see, **nandito/narito, nandiyan/nariyan, nandiyan/nariyan** are equivalent to saying *is here, is there,* or *is over there.* None of these sentences use the *be*-verb (or even have a verb at all). However, these locational adverbs help supply the meaning of "be" in these sentences.

Now compare the sentences above with the following sentences.

Nag-aaral ako <u>rito</u> sa Maynila.	*I study here in Manila.*
<u>Diyan</u> ako nakatira.	*I live there.*
Magtatrabaho ako <u>roon</u> sa New York.	*I will work over there in New York.*

In these sentences, **rito, diyan** and **roon**, are used to mean *here, there, over there* in sentences with verbs.

See if you can answer the following questions. Notice that for **saan** questions, you need to answer using **dito/rito, doon/roon,** and **diyan/riyan**. For **nasaan** questions, answer with **narito, nariyan,** or **naroon**.

1. Question: **Nasaan ka?** *Where are you?*

   Answer: **Narito ako.** *I am here.*

2. Question: **Nasaan ang bahay mo?** *Where is your house?*

   Answer: _____ **ang bahay ko sa.** Los Angeles.

3. Question: **Saan ka nag-aaral?** Where do you study?

   Answer: **Nag-aaral ako** _____ **sa.** UCLA.

4. Question: **Saan ka magtatrabaho?** *Where will you work?*

   Answer: _____.

SUMMING UP

Let us review what you have just learned in this chapter.

Talk/write about the people or objects in your house and where they are. Practice using words for rooms of a house.

_____

_____

_____

_____

_____

_____

CHAPTER 6

Do you have a pen?
May bolpen ka ba?

In this chapter, we will learn words for common objects, adjectives including colors, as well as review and expand the use of possessive pronouns, demonstrative pronouns, and the question words **alin** (*which*) and **kanino** (*whose*).

Asking for a Pen

In this dialogue, Mr. Tolentino and Ralph are in the conference room. Mr. Tolentino forgot his pen in his office and would like to borrow Ralph's pen. Note that Ralph uses honorifics or polite words such as **ho** and **oho**.

Prepare by studying or reviewing the following words, phrases, and sentences.

may [pronounced mai]/ **mayroon** [mai-ro-on]/ **meron** [me-ron]	*have*
bolpen	*ballpoint pen/pen*
may bolpen	ballpoint pen + have *has/have a ballpoint pen*
May bolpen ka ba?	Have + ballpoint pen + you + **ba**? *Do you have a ballpoint pen?*
Mayroon.	*I do have./I have a ...* (informal)
ho/po	honorifics (words used to show respect)
Mayroon ho.	have + **ho**. *I do have./I have a ...* (formal)
Heto.	*Here it is./Here you are.*
Salamat.	*Thank you.*
Walang anuman.	*You're welcome.* (literally, *no matter*)

 **DIALOGUE A**

Mr. Tolentino : **May bolpen ka ba?** *Do you have a pen?*
Ralph   : **Mayroon ho. Heto.** *I do. Here it is.*

Mr. Tolentino : **Salamat.** *Thank you.*

Ralph : **Walang anuman.** *You are welcome.*

VOCABULARY AND GRAMMAR

Learn these words for common objects from the house, classroom, and office.

lapis	*pencil*
papel	*paper*
libro	*book*
kuwaderno/notebook	*notebook*
bote ng tubig	*water bottle*
pamaypay	*fan*
panyo	*handkerchief*
telepono	*phone*
susi	*key*
payong	*umbrella*
kompyuter	*computer*
pitaka	*wallet*
kalendaryo	*calendar*
bentilador	*electric fan*

Some grammar pointers on the use of **may**, **mayroon**, and **meron**:

1. **Meron** is a variation of **mayroon**, which is the standard Tagalog word. It is used exactly in the same way that **mayroon** is used.

2. When using **mayroon** or **meron** in a sentence, we pair them with the linker **na**, thus forming a contraction:

mayroong	*have* (**mayroon** + **na**)
merong	*have* (**meron** + **na**)

Mayroong libro si Melissa.	*Have book* **si** *Melissa.*
Merong libro si Melissa.	*Have book* **si** *Melissa.*

3. Although **mayroon** and **may** have exactly the same meaning, there are two differences in their use. First, in a sentence, the word order changes for **may** and **mayroon/meron** when pronouns are used. The pronoun comes after **mayroon**, and **na** is attached to the pronoun:

akong	*I* (**ako** + **na**)

kang	*you* (**ka** + **na**)
siyang	*him/her* (**siya** + **na**)
May libro siya.	*Have book he/she. Have he/she book.*

Second, **mayroon/meron** can be used on their own as complete sentences. **May** cannot stand on its own.

Mayroon.	*I do have.* (literally, *Have.*)

Study the following sentences:

Melissa has a book.

May libro si Melissa.	Have + book + **si** + Melissa.
Mayroong libro si Melissa.	Have + **na** + book + **si** + Melissa.
Merong libro si Melissa.	Have + **na** + book + **si** + Melissa.

My mother has a phone.

May telepono ang nanay ko.	Have + phone + **ang** + mother + my.
Mayroong telepono ang nanay ko.	Have + **na** + phone + **ang** + mother + my.
Merong telepono si Ralph.	Have + **na** + phone + **ang** + mother + my.

I have a book.

May libro ako.	Have + book + I.
Mayroon akong libro.	Have + I + **na** + book.
Meron akong libro.	Have + I + **na** + book.

He/she has a phone.

May telepono siya.	Have + phone + he/she.
Mayroon siyang telepono.	Have + he/she + **na** + phone.
Meron siyang telepono.	Have + he/she + **na** + phone.

Notes on ba:

For Yes/No questions, the particle **ba** is used. Study the following examples to see how the placement of **ba** varies depending on whether the sentence uses a common noun or a proper noun (name of a person, place, etc.).

May pamaypay ka ba?	Have + fan + you + **ba**? *Do you have a fan?*
May pamaypay ba si Sarah?	Have + fan + **ba** + **si** + Sarah? *Does Sarah have a fan?*

When using **ba** with **mayroon** or **meron**, attach the linker **na** (contracted as **ng**) to **ba** to form the word **bang**.

Mayroon ka bang pamaypay?	Have + you + **ba** + **na** + fan? *Do you have a fan?*
Mayroon bang pamaypay si Sarah?	Have + **ba** + **na** + fan + si Sarah? *Does Sarah have a fan?*

Here are answers you can give.

Mayroon.	*I do.* (Literally, *Have.*)
Oo. (pronounced o-o)	*Yes.*
Wala.	*I don't.* (Literally, *Don't have.*)
May pamaypay ako.	Have + fan + I. *I have a fan.*
Oo, mayroon akong pamaypay.	Yes + have + **na** + fan. *Yes, I have a fan.*
Wala akong pamaypay.	Don't have + I + **na** + fan. *I don't have a fan.*
Walang pamaypay si Sarah.	Don't have + **na** + fan + **si** + Sarah. *Sarah doesn't have a fan.*

Remember, we don't use **hindi** (*no*). To indicate non-possession, we use the word **wala**.

QUESTION AND ANSWER PRACTICE

Ask and answer the following questions to practice **mayroon/may/meron** and **wala** using the cues below.

Ralph – **telepono**
Mr. Tolentino – folder
Sarah – iPad
Melissa – **panyo**

1. Question: **May telepono ba si Ralph?**

   Answer: **Oo,** _____ **si Ralph.**

2. Question: _____?

   Answer: **Oo, may folder si Mr. Tolentino.**

3. Question: **Mayroon bang Ipad si Sarah?**

   Answer: _____.

4. Question: _____ **ba si** _____?

   Answer: **Walang telepono si Melissa.**

5. Question: **Mayroon ka bang susi?**

   Answer: _____.

6. Question: _____?

   Answer: **Wala akong kompyuter.**

Borrowing a Folder

Mr. Tolentino and Ralph are still in the conference room.

Study how to form sentences expressing permission and possibility, and the use of the question word **alin** (*which*).

puwede	*can/may/might*
puwede ba akong	can + **ba** + I + **na**. *Can I?*
humiram	*borrow*
Puwede ba akong humiram ng folder?	Can + **ba** + I + **na** + borrow + **ng** + folder? *Can I borrow a folder?*
alin	*which*
aling	*which* (**alin** + **na**)
Aling folder	Which + **na** + folder? *Which folder?*
iyon	*that*
asul	*blue*
asul na folder	blue + **na** + folder *blue folder*
Iyong asul na folder.	That + **na** + blue + folder. *That blue folder.*

🔘 **DIALOGUE B**

Mr Tolentino	:	**Puwede ba akong humiram ng folder?** *Can I borrow a folder?*
Ralph	:	**Aling folder po?** *Which folder?*
Mr Tolentino	:	**Iyong asul na folder.** *That blue folder.*
Ralph	:	**Heto po.** *Here.*
Mr Tolentino	:	**Salamat.** *Thank you.*
Ralph	:	**Walang anuman.** *You're welcome.*

VOCABULARY AND PRACTICE

In the dialogue above, you learned the word **asul** (*blue*). Here are the names for some other colors. In some instances, there are two or more words for the same color. For example, the Spanish-derived word for blue is **asul**, but the indigenous word is **bughaw**.

pula	*red*
puti	*white*
itim	*black*
luntian/berde	*green*
dilaw	*yellow*
kayumanggi/kulay kape	*brown*
kulay	*color*
kulay abo	*gray* (literally, *the color of ash*)
rosas	*pink*
lila	*purple/violet/lavender*
kulay kahel	*orange*
kulay ginto	*gold*
kulay pilak	*silver*

Here are some words and phrases you can use to ask and answer questions about colors.

anong (contraction of **ano** + **na**)	*what*
anong kulay	what + **na** + color. *What color?*
Anong kulay ang bag mo?	What + color + **ang** + bag + your? *What is the color of your bag?*
Itim ang bag ko.	Black + **ang** + bag + my. *My bag is black.*

QUESTION AND ANSWER PRACTICE

Now, ask and answer questions using the patterns below:

Question: **Anong kulay ang ballpen mo?**
What is the color of your ballpoint pen
Answer: **Asul ang ballpen ko.** *My ballpoint pen is blue.*

Question: **Anong kulay ang** _____ **mo?**
What is the color of your <u>object</u>?
Answer: _____ **ang** _____ **ko.** *My <u>object</u> is <u>color</u>.*

1. Question: **Anong kulay ang bag mo?** *What is the color of your bag?*

   Answer: _____ **ang bag ko.** *My bag is* _____.

2. Question: **Anong kulay ang libro mo?**

   Answer: _____.

3. Question: _____?

   Answer: **Puti ang pamaypay ko.**

4. Question: _____?

   Answer: **Dilaw ang payong ko.**

> **VOCABULARY AND CULTURE TIP (Color Confusion)** You might hear Filipinos refer to brown sugar as **pulang asukal** (*red sugar*), or to gray hair as **puting buhok** (*white hair*). This is not wrong, just different.

GRAMMAR AND PRACTICE

Linking Adjectives and Nouns

To link adjectives and nouns, we use the linker **na**. Here are a few reminders regarding the use of linkers.

1. We can exchange the word order of adjectives and nouns. For example:

itim na bag   black + na + bag *black bag*
bag na itim   bag + na + black *black bag*

2. When the linker **na** follows a word that ends with a vowel, we can contract that word. For example:

pula + na = pulang   red + na *red*
pulang bag   red + na + bag *red bag*

The Question Word "**Alin**" (Which)

In this chapter, we are studying the question word **alin** (*which*). Study the ways below in which we can use **alin** in sentences.

Aling bag?   Which + na + bag? *Which bag?*
Alin ang bag mo?   Which + ang + bag + your? *Which is your bag?*

o	*or*
ang asul na bag o **ang pulang bag**	**ang** + blue + **na** + bag + or + **ang** + red + **na** + bag. *blue bag or red bag*
Alin ang bag mo, **ang asul na bag** **o ang pulang bag?**	Which + **ang** + bag + your, + ang blue + **na** + bag, or + **ang** + red + **na** + bag? *Which is your bag, the blue bag, or the red bag?*
iyo	*yours*
Aling bag ang iyo, **ang asul na bag** **o ang pulang bag?**	Which + **na** + bag + **ang** + yours, + **ang** + blue + **na** + bag + or + **ang** + red + **na** + bag? *Which bag is yours, the blue bag or the red bag?*

POSSESSIVE PRONOUNS AND ADJECTIVES

This prompts us to study the possessives **mo** and **iyo**. You have learned about possessive pronouns in Chapters 1 and 3, and have practiced **ko** (*my*) and **akin** (*my, mine*). But when do we use **mo** and **iyo**? Since both mean *your*, what is the difference between the two words? We use **mo** after the noun, and use **iyo** before the noun.

Which is your bag?

Alin ang bag mo?	Which + **ang** + bag + your?
Alin ang iyong bag?	Which + **ang** + your + **na** + bag?

We can also use **iyo** alone to mean *yours*. We cannot use **mo** in this way. Like **iyo**, both **akin** and **kanya** can be used as possessive pronouns. For example:

Alin ang iyo?	Which is yours?
Alin ang akin?	Which is mine?
Alin ang kanya?	Which is his/hers?

Study the possessive pronoun/adjective chart below:

	Before a noun	**After a noun**
1st Person	**akin** *my/mine*	**ko** *my*
2nd Person	**iyo** *your, yours*	**mo** *your*
3rd Person	**kanya** *his/her, his/hers*	**niya** *his/her*

QUESTION AND ANSWER PRACTICE

Study the following examples, and then ask and answer questions using the cues provided.

Question: **Aling bag ang nasa ibabaw ng mesa?**
Which bag is on top of the table?

Answer: **Ang itim na bag ang nasa ibabaw ng mesa.**
The black bag is on top of the table.

Question: **Alin ang bag mo?** *Which is your bag?*

Answer: **Ang berdeng bag ang bag ko.** *The green bag is my bag.*

black pencil – yours
red pencil – his/hers
blue book – mine
yellow book – his/hers

1. Question: **Alin ang lapis niya?**

    Answer: **Ang _____ na lapis ang lapis _____.**

2. Question: **Alin ang libro ko?**

    Answer: _____.

3. Question: _____?

    Answer: **Ang dilaw na libro ang libro niya.**

4. Question: _____?

    Answer: **Ang itim na lapis ang lapis mo.**

Whose folder is this?

kanino	*whose*
kaninong	whose + **na** *whose*
ito	*this* (demonstrative pronoun)
Kaninong folder ito	Whose + **na** + folder + this? *Whose folder is this?*

folder ko	*my folder*
iyan	*that*
Folder ko iyan.	Folder + my + that. *That is my folder.* (informal)
Folder ko po iyan.	Folder + my + **po** + that. *That is my folder.* (formal)
Alin ang folder ko?	Which + **ang** + folder + my? *Which is my folder?*

malaki	*big*
malaking	big + **na** *big*
malaking folder	big + **na** + folder *big folder*

Mr. Tolentino	:	**Kaninong folder ito?** *Whose folder is this?*
Roland	:	**Folder ko po iyan.** *That is my folder.*
Mr. Tolentino	:	**Alin ang folder ko?** *Which is my folder?*
Roland	:	**Iyong malaking folder po.** *The big folder.*

GRAMMAR

The Question Word "kanino" (*Whose*)

Now, let us study the use of the question word **kanino** (*whose*). There are two ways by which we can ask **kanino** questions. In the dialogue above, the word **kanino** is followed by the linker **na**, and is contracted to form **kaninong** (**na** becomes **ng**).

kanino + na = kaninong	whose + **na**
Kaninong folder ito?	Whose + **na** + folder + this?
	Whose folder is this?

Another way is to use the marker **ang** after **kanino**. **Ang**, as you know by now, tells us that the folder is the focus of the sentence.

Kanino ang folder	Whose + **ang** + folder + na + this?
na ito?	Whose + **ang** + folder + that + this?
	(literally, *Whose is the folder that is this?*)
	Whose folder is this?

In the sentence above, **na** is used as the relative pronoun, *that*. We will discuss relative pronouns in a later chapter.

Here are a few more examples.

Kaninong bag ito?	Whose + **na** + bag + this? *Whose bag is this?*
Kanino ang bag na ito?	Whose + **ang** + bag + that + this?
	(literally, *Whose is the bag that is this?*)
	Whose bag is this?

Adjectives

In Chapter 4, you studied adjectives to describe people. Now, let us study adjectives to describe objects, and demonstrative pronouns.

maliit	*small*
malaki	*big*
maganda	*beautiful*
pangit	*ugly*
maiksi*	*short*
mahaba	*long*
manipis*	*thin*
makapal*	*thick*

*Only for objects

Study how these adjectives are used in the following questions and answers. Note that when the adjective ends with a vowel, the word **na** is attached to the adjective and changes into **ng**.

Question: **Kaninong libro ang malaking libro?**
Whose book is the big book?

Answer: **Libro ko ang malaking libro.**
The big book is my book.

Question: **Kanino ang makapal na libro na ito?**
Whose thick book is this?
(literally, *Whose is the thick book that is this?*)

Answer: **Libro ko ang makapal na libro.**
The thick book is my book.

Demonstrative Pronouns

Determine which demonstrative pronouns to use by the distance of the object to the speaker or the person being addressed.

ito   *this* (*close to the speaker*)
iyan   *that* (closer to the person addressed)
iyon   *that* (far from both the speaker and the person addressed)

Practice these sentences using the question word **kanino** (*whose*) as well as the markers **kay** (for proper nouns) and **sa** (for common nouns).

Question: **Kaninong folder iyan?**
            Whose folder is that?
Answer: **Akin ito.**
            This is mine.

Question: **Kaninong libro iyon?**
            Whose book is that?
Answer: **Kay Maria iyon.**
            That is Maria's.

Question: **Kaninong pamaypay ito?**
            Whose book is this?
Answer: **Sa nanay ko iyan.**
            That is my mother's.

QUESTION AND ANSWER PRACTICE

Ask and answer questions using the cues below.

big book – your sister's
short pencil – Melissa's
small notebook – Sarah's
thick folder – your friend's

1. Question: **Kaninong libro ang malaking libro?**

   Answer: **Sa** _____ **ko ang** _____.

2. Question: **Kanino ang maiksing lapis?**

   Answer: **Kay** _____.

3. Question: **Kaninong notebook ang** _____?

    Answer: _____.

4. Question: _____?

    Answer: **Sa kaibigan ko ang makapal na folder.**

SUMMING UP

Let us review what you have just learned in Chapter 6.

Talk/write about the things inside your bag. Describe them using the colors and adjectives you have learned. Then, talk about objects in your room. Use the demonstrative pronouns **ito, iyan,** and **iyon** to refer to them.

_____

_____

_____

_____

_____

_____

_____

_____

_____

_____

CHAPTER 7

How many pens do you have?
Ilan ang bolpen mo?

In this chapter, we will study how to make requests. We will also study numbers and plural forms.

I Have Three Pens

Ralph and Mr. Tolentino are in the conference room. This is a variation of the dialogue you learned in Chapter 6.

Study the following words, phrases and sentences. Remember that in Tagalog root words are base words, and we add affixes to these words to change their meaning.

hiram	*borrow* (root word, also means *lend*)
humiram	*to borrow* (also, *borrowed*)
pa-	*please* (prefix)
pahiram	*please lend*
ng	marker (used to introduce a noun)
Pahiram ng bolpen mo.	Please lend + **ng** + pen + your. *Please lend me your pen.*
naman	expression used for emphasis
Pahiram naman ng bolpen mo.	Please lend + **naman** + **ng** + pen + your. *Please lend me your pen.*
sauli	*return* (root word)
isasauli	*will return*
mamaya	*later*
Isasauli ko mamaya.	Return + I + later. *I will return it later.*
huwag	*don't*
na	used here to mean *already*
Huwag na ho.	*Your don't have to.* (literally, *Don't already.*) (formal)
tatlo	*three*
Tatlo ang bolpen ko.	Three + **ang** + pen + my. *I have three pens.*

 **DIALOGUE A**

Mr. Tolentino	:	**Pahiram naman ng bolpen mo.**
		Please lend me your pen.
Ralph	:	**Heto ho.** *Here it is.*
Mr. Tolentino	:	**Isasauli ko mamaya.** *I will return it later.*
Ralph	:	**Huwag na ho. Tatlo ho ang bolpen ko.**
		You don't have to. I have three pens.

VOCABULARY AND PRACTICE

Numbers

First, let us study numbers. There are two ways of counting in Tagalog: the indigenous way, and the Spanish-derived way. Filipinos use both. However, for objects people tend to use the indigenous numbers, and they tend to tell the time using the Spanish-derived numbers.

	Tagalog	Spanish–derived
1	isa	uno
2	dalawa	dos
3	tatlo	tres
4	apat	kuwatro
5	lima	singko
6	anim	sais
7	pito	siyete
8	walo	otso
9	siyam	nuwebe
10	sampu	diyes
11	labing-isa	onse
12	labindalawa	dose
13	labintatlo	trese
14	labing-apat	katorse
15	labinlima	kinse
16	labing-anim	disisais
17	labimpito	disisiyete
18	labingwalo	disiotso
19	labinsiyam	disinuwebe
20	dalawampu	beinte
21	dalawampu't isa	beinte-uno
22	dalawampu't dalawa	beinte-dos
30	tatlumpu	treinta

40	apatnapu	kuwarenta
50	limampu	singkuwenta
60	animnapu	sisenta
70	pitumpu	sitenta
80	walumpu	otsenta
90	siyamnapu	nobenta
100	sandaan	siyento
1000	sanlibo	mil
10,000	sampung libo	diyes mil
100,000	sandaang libo	siyento mil
1,000,000		isang milyon
1,000,000,000		isang bilyon

SENTENCE CONSTRUCTION AND GRAMMAR

Here are a few reminders when using words for ownership (**may/may-roon/meron**) and numbers:

1. The question word for *how many* is **ilan**.
2. To show ownership, we use the markers **ni** (for proper nouns) and **ng** (for common nouns).
3. As you learned in Chapter 4, we use the word **mga** to make plurals. However. we do not use **mga** and numbers at the same time. Also, because numbers are adjectives, remember to use the linker **na** to connect the number and the noun. If the number ends in a vowel, **na** is contracted into **ng**.

For example:

apat + na = apat na libro   *four books*
lima + na = limang libro   *five books*

CORRECT: **Mayroon akong limang libro.** *I have two books.*
WRONG: **Mayroon akong mga limang libro.**

4. When asking "How many ____ do you have?," we do not need to pluralize the noun.

Study the following sentences.

Ilan ang lapis mo?   How many + **ang** + pencil + have?
How many pencils do you have?

Mayroon akong limang lapis.   Have + I + **na** + five + **na** pencils.
I have five pencils.

Lima ang lapis ko.	Five + **ang** + pencil + my. *I have five pencils.*
Ilan ang libro mo?	*How many books do you have?*
Mayroon akong tatlong libro.	*I have three books.*
Tatlo ang libro ko.	*I have three books.*
Ilan ang libro ni Melissa?	*How many books does Melissa have?*
Apat ang libro ni Melissa.	*Melissa has four books.*
Ilan ang bote ng tubig ng kapatid mo?	*How many water bottles does your brother/ sister have?*
Dalawa ang bote ng tubig ng kapatid ko.	*My brother/sister has two water bottles.*

QUESTION AND ANSWER PRACTICE

Ask and answer questions using the cues below.

Sarah – 2 fans
Melissa – 3 telephones
Ralph – 10 folders
your friend – 5 bags
you – 6 water bottles

1. Question: **Ilan ang pamaypay ni Sarah?**

   Answer: _____ **ang pamaypay ni Sarah**.

2. Question: **Ilan ang telepono ni Melissa?**

   Answer: _____ **ang** _____ **ni** _____.

3. Question: Ilan ang folders ni Ralph?

   Answer: _____.

4. Question: _____ **ang** _____ **ng** _____ **mo?**

   Answer: **Lima ang bags ng kaibigan ko.**

5. Question: _____?

   Answer: **Anim ang bote ng tubig ko.**

GRAMMAR AND PRACTICE

Requests: Using the Affix "Pa-"

The affix **pa-** is equivalent to the word *please.*

You just learned **hiram** (*borrow/lend,* root word) and **pahiram** (*please lend*). Here are some other words that may be useful:

hingi   *give* (root word)
pahingi   *please give me*
abot   *reach/pass* (root word)
paabot   *please pass me*

The words above can be used when asking a favor. Study the following sentences:

Pahiram ng libro mo.   Please borrow + **ng** + book + your.
                              Please let me borrow your book.
Pahingi ng papel.   Please give + **ng** + paper. *Please give me some paper.*
Paabot ng lapis ko.   Please + pass + **ng** + pencil + my.
                              Please pass me my pencil.

When giving an object to someone, some people say "**Heto.** (*Here you are.*)"

Now, let us practice these words by making dialogues for the following situations.

Situation 1 You want your sister to reach the salt shaker and give it to you.

You   : _____ **ng salt shaker.**

Your sister   : _____.

Situation 2 You want your friend to lend you a pen.

You   : _____?

Your friend : _____.

Situation 3 You want to ask your mother for two pencils.

You   : _____?

Your mother : _____.

Verbs: An introduction to Focuses, and Verb Affixes

In this chapter, we will explain verb focus and introduce the actor and object focus. We will also show how to conjugate the new verbs you have learned: **hiram**, **hingi**, and **abot**.

Here are some points to remember:

1. What does "focus" mean?

In Tagalog, verb affixes are used based on the focus of the sentence. Focus, according to Teresita Ramos, is "the grammatical relationship that exists between the verb and the verbal complement."[1] Basically, to determine focus, we can ask, "What is given emphasis in the sentence?"

Focus can also be understood when compared to voice. In the English language, a sentence uses the active voice when the subject does the action expressed by the verb. On the other hand, a sentence uses the passive voice when the subject is the receiver of the action.

However, we use the term "focus" instead of "voice" in Tagalog grammar because there are five possible focuses (actor, object, locative or directional, benefactive, and instrumental) for Tagalog verbs.

2. What is the "actor" focus?

An actor-focus sentence gives emphasis to the <u>doer</u> of the action. These sentences can be thought of as responses to questions with **sino** (*who*).

Question: **Sino ang humiram ng folder?** *Who borrowed the folder?*
Answer: **Si Mr. Tolentino ang humiram ng folder.**
  Mr. Tolentino borrowed the folder.

Here are other actor-focus sentences.

Question: **Sino ang nag-abot ng folder?** *Who passed the folder?*

Answers: _____.

Nag-abot si Ralph ng folder kay Mr. Tolentino.	Passed + **si** + Ralph + **ng** + folder + to + Mr. Tolentino.
	Ralph passed a folder to Mr. Tolentino.
Nag-abot ang secretary ng folder kay Mr. Tolentino.	Passed + **ang** + secretary + **ng** + folder + to + Mr. Tolentino.
	The secretary passed a folder to Mr. Tolentino.

---

[1] Ramos, Teresita. *Tagalog Structures.* p. 88.

Nag-abot ako ng	Passed + I + **ng** + folder + to +
folder kay Mr. Tolentino.	Mr. Tolentino. *I passed a folder to*
	Mr. Tolentino.

3. **How do we know that the focus of the sentence is on the actor (or the doer of the action)?**

Through clues or subject markers. In the sentences above, **si** (marker for names or proper nouns), **ang** (marker for nouns), and the subject pronoun **ako** point to "Ralph," "the secretary," and "I," respectively, as the actors.

4. **How can we conjugate verbs using the affixes "mag-" and "-um-"?**

In Chapter 3, we introduced the verb conjugations for what can be called **mag** verbs. The prefix **mag-** is used for the contemplated aspect of the verb (similar to the English future tense), while its variation, the prefix **nag-** is used for both the completed aspect (similar to the English past tense) and the incompleted aspect (similar to the English present tense). The prefix **mag-** is one of two prefixes (the other one is **um-** which we will discuss later), most commonly used when the focus is on the actor or the doer of the action. Here is a brief review of how **mag** verbs are formed, showing how they are used in sentences.

root word – abot

infinitive (used with helping verbs such as *can, want,* and *could*) and
   imperative forms – **mag-** + root word = **mag-abot**
completed aspect – **nag-** + root word = **nag-abot**
incompleted – **nag-** + first syllable of root word + root word = **nag-aabot**
contemplated – **mag-** + first syllable of root word + root word = **mag-aabot**

puwede	*can*
puwede ako	*I can*
puwede akong mag-abot	can + I + **na** + pass. *I can pass*
Puwede akong mag-abot ng folder.	Can + I + **na** + pass + **ng** + folder. *I can pass a folder.*
Nag-abot ako ng folder.	Passed + I + **ng** + folder. *I passed a folder.*
Nag-aabot ako ng folder.	Passing + I + **ng** + folder. *I am passing a folder.*
Mag-aabot ako ng folder.	Will pass + I + **ng** + folder. *I will pass a folder.*

Not all Tagalog verbs use **mag-** prefixes. Some verbs can be called **um-** verbs, as they use **-um-** affixes. There is no specific grammar rule as to when to use **mag-** or **um-**. As such, learners need to remember which affix to use in the verbs. We put the **-um-** affix before the first vowel of the root word. Here are the formulas and a few examples.

root word – hiram

infinitive/imperative form – **-um-** + root word = **humiram**
completed aspect – **-um-** + root word = **humiram**
incompleted – first two syllables of the completed aspect + root word =
   humihiram
contemplated – first syllable of root + root word = **hihiram**

Puwede akong humiram ng folder.	Can + I + **na** + borrow + **ng** + folder. *I can borrow a folder.*
Humiram ako ng folder.	Borrowed + I + **ng** + folder. *I borrowed a folder.*
Humihiram ako ng folder.	Borrowing + I + **ng** + folder. *I am borrowing a folder.*
Hihiram ako ng folder.	Will borrow + I + **ng** + folder.

5. What is the object focus?

Sentences where the focus is on the <u>object</u> can be thought of as responses to questions using the word **ano** (*what*). In these sentences, emphasis is given to the "object" or "goal" of the action.

Question:	**Ano ang hiniram ni Mr. Tolentino?** *What did Mr. Tolentino borrow?*
Answer:	**Folder ang hiniram ni Mr. Tolentino.** *It is a folder that Mr. Tolentino borrowed.*

One of the most common affixes for object focus verbs is the **-in-** affix. We put the affix before the first syllable of the root word.

Here are the formulas for **-in-** verbs.

root word – hiramin

infinitive/imperative form – root word + **-in** = **hiramin**
completed aspect – **-in-** before the first vowel of the root word + root word
   = **hiniram**
incompleted – first two syllables of the completed aspect + root word =
   hinihiram

contemplated – first syllable of root + root word + -**in** = **hihiramin**

Puwede kong hiramin ang folder.	Can + I + **na** + borrow + marker folder. *A folder is what I can borrow.*
Folder ang hiniram ko.	Folder + **ang** + borrowed + I. *A folder is what I borrowed.*
Folder ang hinihiram ko.	Folder + **ang** + borrowing + I. *A folder is what I am borrowing.*
Folder ang hihiramin ko.	Folder + **ang** + will borrow + I. *A folder is what I will borrow.*

6. **How do we know that the focus of a sentence is the object (or the receiver of the action)?**

Note the marker **ang**. In the sentences above, it is closer to the object ("the folder"). Also, notice the object pronoun **ko**, used here instead of the subject pronoun **ako**.

Compare the following sentences.

Humiram ng folder si Mr. Tolentino.	*Mr. Tolentino borrowed a folder.*
Folder ang hiniram ni Mr. Tolentino.	*A folder was borrowed by Mr. Tolentino.*

In the first sentence, **si** marks Mr. Tolentino, the actor, as the focus of the sentence, while **ng** marks folder and tells us that it is not the focus. In the second sentence, **ang** marks the folder as the focus, while the marker **ni** tells us that Mr. Tolentino is not the focus. To review:

si subject marker for names or proper nouns
ang subject marker for common nouns
ni object marker for names or proper nouns
ng object marker for common nouns

Here are two tables for the verbs we are studying in this chapter.

Actor Focus

VERB (Root)	INF/IMP	COMPLETED	INCOMPLETED	CONTEMPLATED
hiram	humiram	humiram	humihiram	hihiram
hingi	humingi	humingi	humihingi	hihingi
abot	mag-abot	nag-abot	nag-aabot	mag-aabot

Object Focus

VERB	INF/IMP	COMPLETED	INCOMPLETED	CONTEMPLATED
hiram	hiramin	hiniram	hinihiram	hihiramin
hingi	hingin	hiningi	hinihingi	hihingin
abot	abutin	inabot	inaabot	aabutin

Study how these verbs are used in the following sentences:

Humiram ako ng libro.   Borrowed + I + **ng** + book.
(actor focus)   *I borrowed a book.*

Libro ang hiniram ko.   Book + **ang** + borrowed + I.
(object focus)   *A book is what I borrowed.*

Gusto kong humiram   Want + I + **na** + borrow + **ng** + book.
ng libro.   *I want to borrow a book.*

Humingi ako ng papel.   Asked + I + **ng** + paper.
(actor focus)   *I asked for paper.*

Papel ang hiningi ko.   Paper + **ang** + asked + I.
(object focus)   *Paper is what I asked for.*

Nag-aabot si Ralph   Passing + **si** + Ralph + **ng** + folder +
ng folder kay   to + Mr. Tolentino.
Mr. Tolentino.   *Ralph is passing a folder to Mr Tolentino.*
(actor focus)

Folder ang inaabot   Folder + **ang** + passing + **ni** + Ralph + **kay** +
ni Ralph kay   Mr. Tolentino. *A folder is what Ralph is passing*
Mr. Tolentino.   *to Mr. Tolentino.*
(object focus)

VOCABULARY AND GRAMMAR TIP (Translations) Some words such as **abot**
do not have an exact English translation. **Abot** really means "reach for something." Yet the phrase **paabot ng salt shaker** should be translated as "Pass me
the salt shaker." Bear in mind – a language embodies a culture, and all cultures
are different, so some words exist in one culture but do not exist in another.
For example, in Tagalog, we do not have words for "alienation" or "apathy"
although we can have something similar for the latter—**walang pakialam** (*lack
of concern*). Why? Because indigenous communities were close-knit and people
were interdependent.

Borrowing Books

Ralph, who is now in his third month in Manila, is calling his new friend, Melissa, to ask about borrowing books from her. In this conversation, we will study the different aspects of the verbs **hiram**, **hingi**, and **abot**, as well as **puwede** (*can/may*) and the plural form for objects.

puwede	*can/may*
puwede ko bang makausap	*can I speak to*
Puwede ko bang makausap si Melissa?	Can + I + **bang** + talk + **si** + Melissa? *Can I speak to Melissa?*
puwede ba akong humiram	*can I borrow*
Puwede ba akong humiram ng libro?	Can + **ba** + I + **na** + borrow + **ng** + book? *Can I borrow a book?*
anong klase	*what kind*
Anong klaseng libro?	What + kind + **na** + book? *What kind of book?*
tungkol	*about*
kasaysayan	*history*
kasaysayan ng Pilipinas	*Philippine history*
tungkol sa kasaysayan ng Pilipinas	*about Philippine history*
Iyong tungkol sa kasaysayan.	That + about + **sa** + history. *One that's about history.*
hiniram	*borrowed*
Hiniram ko sa library.	Borrowed + I + **at** + library. *I borrowed (the books) from the library.*
gusto	*want*
gusto mo bang pumunta	*do you want to go*
Gusto mo bang pumunta sa bahay ko?	Want + you + **bang** + go + to + house + my? *Would you like to come to my house?*

 DIALOGUE B

RALPH : **Hello. Puwede ko bang makausap si Melissa?**
Hello. Can I speak to Melissa?

MELISSA : **Si Melissa ito.** *This is Melissa.*

RALPH : **Si Ralph ito. Puwede ba akong humiram ng libro?**
This is Ralph. Can I borrow a book?

MELISSA : **Siyempre. Anong klaseng libro?** *Of course. What kind of book?*

RALPH : **Iyong tungkol sa kasaysayan ng Pilipinas.**
One that's about Philippine history.

MELISSA : **Mayroon akong apat na libro. Hiniram ko sa library. Gusto mo bang pumunta sa bahay ko?** *I have four books. I borrowed them from the library. Do you want to come to my house?*

RALPH : **Sige.** *Okay.*

VOCABULARY

Here are related words and phrases that may be useful to you.

puwede ba akong humingi	*can I ask*
puwede ba akong magtanong	*can I ask a question*
siyempre	*of course*
tanong	*question*
lipunan	*society*
lipunang Filipino	*Philippine society*
siyensiya	*science*
panitikan	*literature*
panitikang Filipino	*Philippine literature*
matematika	*mathematics*
gusto mo bang humiram	*do you want to borrow*
gusto mo bang humingi	*do you want to ask*
gusto mo bang magtanong	*do you want to ask a question*

DIALOGUE PRACTICE

Let us practice the words and phrases you have learned. Make dialogues according to the following situations.

Practice Situation You want to borrow a book on Philippine society from your friend. She has two books.

YOU : **Puwede ba akong humiram ng libro?**
Can I borrow a book?

YOUR FRIEND : **Siyempre. Anong klaseng libro?**
Of course. What kind of book?

You : **Iyong tungkol sa lipunang Filipino. Ilan ang libro mo?** *One that's about Philippine society. How many books do you have?*

Your friend : **Mayroon akong dalawang libro.** *I have two books.*

Situation 1 Your want to borrow a book on Philippine literature. You friend has four books:

You : **Puwede ba** _____ **ng** _____?

Your friend : _____. **Anong** _____?

You : **Libro** _____?

Your friend : **Mayroon** _____.

Situation 2 You want to ask your friend if she wants to borrow your notes from your science class (**klase**). You have 10 pages of notes.

You : **Gusto mo bang** _____ **ang notes ko para sa klase sa siyensiya?**

Your friend : _____. **Ilang pages ang notes mo?**

You : _____ **pages ang notes ko.**

Situation 3 You want to ask your friend for some extra pens. She has four pens and gives you two pens.

You : _____.

Your friend : **Siyempre. Mayroon akong** _____.

You : **Puwede mo ba akong bigyan ng** _____?

Your friend : _____.

SUMMING UP

Let us review what you have just learned in Chapter 7.

Count the objects around you: pens, pencils, books, pieces of paper, etc. Remember to use the linker **na**. Then write a paragraph using helping verbs.

_____

_____

_____

CHAPTER 8

Would you like some coffee?
Gusto mo ba ng kape?

In this chapter, we are studying words related to food and drink, and practicing the use of verbs with actor and object focus.

At Melissa's House

Ralph is in Melissa's house to borrow some books. She had just baked a cake and would like him to try some.

Here are the words, phrases, and sentences from the dialogue.

kape	*coffee*
tsaa	*tea*
kape o tsaa	*coffee or tea*
keyk	*cake*
gusto mo ba ng	*would you like some*
Gusto mo ba ng kape?	Like + you + **ba** + **ng** + coffee? *Would you like some coffee?*
Gusto mo ba ng kape o tsaa?	*Would you like some coffee or tea?*
abala (accent on the third syllable)	*bother* (root word)
mag-abala	*to be bothered*
na	used in the following ways: to mean *already*; as a linker; and as a relative pronoun
nang	contraction of **na** (already) and **na** (linker)
Huwag ka nang mag-abala.	Don't + you + **nang** + bother. *Please don't bother.*
Sige na.	*Please do this.* (used here as an idiom; it has other meanings)
Sige.	*Okay.*
tikim	*taste* (root word)

tikman	*taste* (imperative form)
Tikman mo ang keyk.	*Taste the cake.*
na	*that* (**na** used here as a relative pronoun)
Tikman mo ang keyk na ginawa ko.	*Taste the cake that I made.*

🔵 **DIALOGUE A**

MELISSA : **Gusto mo ba ng kape o tsaa?** *Would you like some coffee or tea?*

RALPH : **Huwag ka nang mag-abala.** *Please don't bother.*

MELISSA : **Sige na.** *Please.*

RALPH : **Sige.** *Okay.*

MELISSA : **Tikman mo ang keyk na ginawa ko.** *Try some of the cake that I made.*

RALPH : **Salamat.** *Thank you.*

VOCABULARY

Here are some other words related to food and drink that you can use. In some instances, we just use English words such as cookies and sandwich because there are no indigenous words for these food items.

gatas	*milk*
asukal	*sugar*
limon	*lemon*
kalamansi	*calamansi* or *Philippine lime*
honey	*honey*

CULTURE NOTE (Offering Food and Drink) In the Filipino culture, it is customary to decline when offered something. The host is expected to ask again, and the guest then partakes of what is being offered. When hosting people in your home and your guests say "**Huwag ka nang mag-abala**" (*Please don't bother*) or "**Nakakahiya naman**" (*I feel ashamed*) or "**Huwag na lang**" (*Perhaps no*), they don't really mean it. Ask again.

DIALOGUE PRACTICE

Let us practice offering food and drink using the dialogue and vocabulary you have just learned. Remember to use phrases that show the back and forth of declining and offering again.

Situation 1 Your friend is in your house. You are offering tea with Philippine lime and honey. You also want him/her to try your freshly baked cookies.

You   : **Gusto** _____?

Your Friend : **Huwag** _____.

You   : _____.

Your Friend : _____.

You   : _____.

Your Friend : _____.

Situation 2 You are in your classmate's house. She is offering you some orange juice. She also asks you to try the panini sandwich she made.

Your classmate : _____?

You   : _____.

Your classmate : _____.

You   : _____.

Your classmate : _____.

You   : _____.

Situation 3 Your cousin is visiting. You just baked a cake. You want to offer her some coffee with milk and sugar.

You   : _____?

Your cousin : _____.

You   : _____.

Your cousin : _____.

You   : _____.

Your cousin : _____.

GRAMMAR

Review the uses of the word "na"

In the dialogues in this chapter and in previous chapters of this book, you may have noticed the different uses of the word **na**.

Here are some sentences (as well as the chapters where they are from) we have learned and the ways that **na** has been used:

Matanda na ang mga magulang ko. used to mean *already.* Old + already + **ang** + parents + my. *My parents are already old.*

Mayroon ka bang pamaypay? used as a linker. Have + you + **ba** + **na** + fan? *Do you have a fan?*

Kanino ang folder na ito? used as the relative pronoun *that* Whose + **ang** + folder + that + this? *Whose folder is this?*

How much sugar?

In this dialogue, Melissa is giving Ralph a slice of cake. Ralph is also having coffee, and so Melissa would like to know how much sugar and milk he wants.

Study the following words, phrases, and sentences.

kain	*eat* (root word)
kumain	*eat* (imperative form)
muna	*beforehand; first*
Kumain ka muna ng cake.	Eat + you + first + **ng** + cake. *Have some cake.*
gawa	*make* (root word)
gumawa	*made* (used when the focus is on the actor)
nito	*this* (demonstrative pronoun used to replace the object)
nitong (nito + linker na)	*this*
Sino ang gumawa nitong cake?	Who + **ang** + made + this + **na** + cake? *Who made this cake?*
ginawa	*made* (used when the focus is on the object)
Ginawa ko ito.	Made + I + this. *I made this.*
sarap	*delicious* (root)
masarap	*delicious* (adjective)
Ang sarap!	**Ang** + delicious! *It's delicious!*
gaano karami	*how much*
gaano karaming asukal	how much + **na** + sugar. *how much sugar*

Gaano karaming asukal ang gusto mo?	How much + **na** + sugar + **ang** + like + you *How much sugar would you like?*
walang gatas	*no milk*
isang kutsarita	*a teaspoon*
lang	*only; just*
Isang kutsaritang asukal lang.	One + teaspoon + **na** + sugar + only. *Just a teaspoon of sugar.*
pa	*more* (used as an adverb; it also means *yet* and *still*)
Gusto mo pa ba ng keyk?	Like + you + more + **ba** + **ng** + cake? *Would you like more cake?*
busog	*full*
na	*already*
Busog na ako.	Full + already + I. *I am full.*
tanghalian	*lunch*
malaki	*huge*
malaking tanghalian	huge + **na** + lunch. *a huge lunch*
Kumain ako ng malaking tanghalian.	Ate + I + **ng** + huge + **na** + lunch. *I ate a huge lunch.*
inom	*drink* (root word)
inumin	*drink* (infinitive form)
gustong inumin	*want to drink*
Mayroon ka pa bang gustong inumin?	Have + you + still + **bang** + want + **na** + drink? *Can I get you something else to drink?*
tubig	*water*
Tubig na lang.	Water + **na** + just. *Just water.*
kung	*if*
kung puwede	if + can. *if it's okay*
Tubig na lang kung puwede.	Water + **na** + just + if + can. *Just water, if it is okay.*

 **DIALOGUE B**

MELISSA : **Kumain ka muna ng keyk.** *Have some cake.*

RALPH : **Salamat, Melissa. Sino ang gumawa nito?**
Thank you, Melissa. Who made this?

MELISSA : **Ginawa ko iyan.** *I made that.*

RALPH : (Tastes the cake.) **Ang sarap!** *It is delicious!*

MELISSA : **Gaano karaming asukal at gatas ang gusto mo?**
How much sugar and milk do you want in your coffee?

RALPH : **Walang gatas. Isang kutsaritang asukal lang.**
No milk. Just a teaspoon of sugar please.

MELISSA : **Gusto mo pa ba ng keyk?** *Would you like more cake?*

RALPH : **Huwag na. Busog na ako. Kumain ako ng malaking tanghalian.** *No. I am full. I ate a huge lunch.*

MELISSA : **Mayroon ka pa bang gustong inumin?** *Can I get you something else?*

RALPH : **Tubig na lang, kung puwede.** *Just water, if it is okay.*

VOCABULARY

Here are yet more words that you can use when talking about food and drink. They are grouped according to function.

Utensils

plato	*plate*	**kutsilyo**	*knife*
platito	*small plate; saucer*	**mangkok**	*bowl*
tinidor	*fork*	**baso**	*glass*
kutsara	*spoon*	**tasa**	*cup*

CULTURE TIP (Snacks) When eating in the Philippines, people are usually just given spoons and forks. You may have to ask for a knife if you would like to use one. Also, some people have a mid-morning snack and a mid-afternoon snack. Why? Well, some scholars have explained that it could be because in the past, farmers who got up very early to work in the fields got hungry at around ten o'clock, so they brought a snack, such as rice cakes. They also needed a lot of energy for farm work so they ate mid-afternoon snacks. Now, in the city, it seems weird to eat at 10 a.m. when one just had breakfast at 7:30 a.m., or to eat five times a day when one does not have to do a lot of physical labor.

Food and Drink

pagkain	*food*
inumin	*drink* (noun)
(accent on the second syllable)/**maiinom**	
tubig	*water*
katas/dyus/juice	*juice*
almusal	*breakfast*
tanghalian	*lunch*
hapunan	*dinner*
merienda/minindal	*snack*

Verbs

kumain	*ate* (actor focus)
Kumain ako ng cake.	*I ate cake.*
kinain	*ate* (object focus)
Cake ang kinain ko.	*I ate cake.*
uminom	*drank* (actor focus)
Uminom ako ng tubig.	*I drank water.*
ininom	*drank* (object focus)
Tubig ang ininom ko.	*Water is what I drank./I drank water.*

Other Words and Expressions

pa	*another/more*
hiwa	*slice*
isa pang hiwa	*another slice*
Gusto mo pa ba ng pie?	*Would you like more pie?*

sa	*at/during*
tuwing	*during; every*
Ano ang kinain mo sa almusal?	What + **ang** + ate + you + at + breakfast? *What did you eat at breakfast?*
Ano ang kinakain mo tuwing tanghalian?	What + **ang** + eat + you + during lunch? *What do you eat during lunch?*
Ano ang kakainin mo sa hapunan?	What + **ang** + will eat + you + at + dinner? *What will you eat at dinner?*
Masarap ang keyk.	*The cake is delicious.*

GRAMMAR AND PRACTICE

Use of the Word "ba"

In previous chapters, you have learned that we use the words **ba** and **bang** (contracted from **ba** and **na**) for yes or no questions.

What is the difference between the following sentences?

Gusto mo ba ng kape?	*Would you like some coffee?*
Gusto mo bang humiram ng libro?	*Would you like to borrow a book?*

In the first sentence we use the object marker **ng** because **kape** (*coffee*) is a noun. In the second sentence, **bang** is formed by the words **ba** and **na**, and **na** here is used to mean "to." Other grammarians might also explain **na**, as used here, is like a relative pronoun, with the sentence having the literal meaning, "Would you like that borrow (you) **ng** book?"

Verb Conjugations

Let us conjugate the new verbs **kain** (eat), **inom** (drink) and **gawa** (make). Study the following chart.

In the case of **gawa**, because it ends in a vowel, we remove the vowel **a** when we conjuagate.

Infinite/Imperative Aspect: **gawa** + **in** = **gawain** = remove the **a** = **gawin**
Completed aspect: **gawa** + -**in**- before the first vowel = **ginawa**
Incompleted aspect : first two syllables of completed aspect + root word
  gawa = **gina** + **gawa** = **ginagawa**
Contemplated aspect: first syllable of root word + root word **gawa** + -**in**-
  (= **ga** + **gawa** + **in** + **gagawain**) + remove the last **a** vowel = **gagawin**

Root	INF/IMP	COMPLETED	INCOMPLETED	CONTEMPLATED
kain (AF)	kumain	kumain	kumakain	kakain
kain (OF)	kainin	kinain	kinakain	kakainin
inom (AF)	uminom	uminom	umiinom	iinom
inom (OF)	inumin	ininom	iniinom	iinumin
gawa (AF)	gumawa	gumawa	gumagawa	gagawa
gawa (OF)	gawin	ginawa	ginagawa	gagawa

AF = action focus; OF = object focus

Let us look at how these verbs are used in the following questions and answers. Note that sometimes there are two ways to answer a question. In some cases, the focus changes in the second answer. In others, just the word order is changed.

1. Question: **Ano ang kinain mo sa almusal?**
   What + **ang** + eat + you + for + breakfast?
   What did you eat for breakfast?

   Answer 1: **Kumain ako ng cereal sa almusal.**
   (actor Ate + I + **ng** + cereal + for + breakfast.
   focus) *I ate cereal for breakfast.*

   Answer 2: **Cereal ang kinain ko sa almusal.**
   (object Cereal + **ang** + ate + I + for + breakfast.
   focus) *Cereal is what I ate for breakfast.*

2. Question: **Saan ka kumakain ng tanghalian?**
   Where + you + eat + **ng** + lunch?
   Where do you eat lunch?

   Answer 1: **Kumakain ako ng tanghalian sa office cafeteria.**
   (word Eat + I + **ng** + lunch + at + office cafeteria.
   order 1) *I eat lunch at the office cafeteria.*

   Answer 2: **Sa office cafeteria ako kumakain ng tanghalian.**
   (word At + office cafeteria + I + eat + **ng** + lunch.
   order 2) *I eat lunch at the office cafeteria.*

3. Question: **Ano ang gusto mong inumin?**
   What + like + you + **na** + to drink?
   What would you like to drink?

   Answer 1: **Gusto kong uminom ng kape.**
   (actor Want /Would like + I + **na** + to drink + **ng** + coffee.
   focus) *I would like to drink coffee.*

   Answer 2: **Kape ang gusto kong inumin.**
   (object Coffee + **ang** + want/would like + I + **na** + to drink.
   focus) *Coffee is what I want to drink.*

4. Question: **Sino ang gagawa ng keyk?**
   Who + **ang** + will make + **ng** + keyk?
   Who will make the cake?

   Answer: **Si Melissa ang gagawa ng keyk.**
   (actor **Si** + Melissa + **ang** + will make + **ng** + cake.
   focus) *Melissa will make the cake.*

5. Question: **Ano ang gagawin ni Melissa?**
            What + **ang** + will make + **ni** + Meliisa?
            What will Melissa make?

Answer 1: **Keyk ang gagawin ni Melissa.**
(object   Cake + **ang** + will make + **ni** + Melissa.
focus)   *A cake is what Melissa will make.*

Answer 2: **Gagawa si Melissa ng cake.**
(actor   Will make + **si** + Melissa + **ng** + cake.
focus)   *Melissa will make a cake?*

Demonstrative Pronouns

In Chapter 6, you learned the demonstrative pronouns **ito** (*this*; object is close to the speaker), **iyan** (*that*; object is close to the person addressed) and **iyon** (*that*; object is far from both the speaker and the person addressed).

In this chapter, we learned the pronoun **nito** (*this*). When do we use **ito** and when do we use **nito**?

1. We use **ito** to replace nouns that are introduced by the marker **ang** in object-focus sentences.

Ano ang ginawa mo?	*What did you make?*
Ginawa ko ang keyk.	*I made the cake.*
Ginawa ko ito.	*I made this.*

2. We use **nito** to replace nouns that are introduced by the marker **ng** in actor-focus sentences.

Sino ang gumawa ng keyk?	*Who made the cake?*
Sino ang gumawa nito?	*Who made this?*
Ako ang gumawa ng keyk.	I + **ang** + made + **ng** + cake.
	It was I who made the cake./ I made the cake.
Ako ang gumawa nito.	I + **ang** + made + this.
	It was I who made this./I made the cake.

3. Like their English equivalent this, both **ito** and **nito** can be used with a noun. However, they are used with the word **na**, which functions in these sentences to mean *that*. **Nito na**, contracted as **nitong**, is put before the noun (cake) while **na ito** is put after the noun (cake).

Sino ang gumawa nitong cake?	Who + **ang** + made + this + that + cake? (literally, *Who made this that is a cake?*) *Who made this cake?*
Sino ang gumawa ng keyk na ito?	Who + **ang** + made + **ng** + cake + that + this? (literally, *Who made the cake that is this?*) *Who made this cake?*

4. To pluralize, we put **mga** before **ito** (*this*). We never pluralize **nito**. When **ito** and **nito** are used with a noun (for example, **mga keyk** or *cakes*), the plural word **mga** is put before the object (**mga keyk**).

The third and fourth sentences show how **mga ito** (these) is used even when replacing a noun marked by **ng** (**ng mga keyk**).

Sino ang gumawa nitong mga keyk?	*Who made these cakes?*
Sino ang gumawa ng mga keyk?	*Who made the cakes?*
Sino ang gumawa ng mga ito?	*Who made these?*
Ako ang gumawa ng mga ito.	*I made these.*
Ginawa ko ang mga ito.	*I made these.*

Sino ang gumawa ng mga keyk na ito?	*Who made these cakes?*
WRONG: **Sino ang gumawa mga nito?**	*Who made these?*

5. Here is a table of demonstrative pronouns. All rules stated apply to **iyan** and **niyan** (*that*; closer to the person being addressed), and **iyon** and **niyon** (*that*; far from both the speaker and the person being addressed).

DEMONSTRATIVE PRONOUNS TABLE

ENGLISH	used to replace nouns marked by "ang"	used to replace nouns marked by "ng"
this *I made this cake.*	**ito** Ginawa ko ang keyk na ito.	**nito** Ako ang gumawa nitong keyk.
this *I made this.*	**ito** Ginawa ko ito.	**nito** Ako ang gumawa nito.
these *I made these cakes.*	**mga** *noun* **na ito** Ginawa ko ang mga keyk na ito.	**nitong mga** *noun* Ako ang gumawa nitong mga keyk.
these *I made these.*	**mga ito** Ginawa ko ang mga ito.	**ito** (plural form only) Ako ang gumawa ng mga ito.
that *I made that cake.*	**iyan** Ginawa ko ang keyk na iyan.	**niyan** Ako ang gumawa niyang keyk.
that *I made that.*	**iyan** Ginawa ko iyan.	**niyan** Ako ang gumawa niyan.
those *I made those cakes.*	**iyan** Ginawa ko ang mga keyk na iyan.	**niyan** Ako ang gumawa niyang mga keyk.
those *I made those.*	**mga iyan** Ginawa ko ang mga iyan.	**mga iyan** (plural only) Ako ang gumawa ng mga iyan.
that (far from both speaker and person addressed) *I made that cake.*	**iyon** Ginawa ko ang keyk na iyon.	**niyon** Ako ang gumawa niyong keyk.
that (far) *I made that.*	**iyon** Ginawa ko iyon.	**niyon** Ako ang gumawa niyon.
those (far) *I made those cakes.*	**mga iyon** Ginawa ko ang mga keyk na iyon.	**mga iyon** Ako ang gumawa niyong mga keyk.
those (far) *I made those.*	**mga iyon** Ginawa ko ang mga iyon.	**mga iyon** (plural only) Ako ang gumawa ng mga iyon.

GRAMMAR PRACTICE

Practice the use of the demonstrative pronouns by filling in the blanks.

1. Question: **Sino ang gumawa ng apple pie na ito?**
   (close to the speaker)

   Answer: **Ginawa ko** _____.

2. Question: **Sino ang gumawa niyan?**
   (close to the person being addressed)

   Answer: **Ako ang** _____.

3. Question: **Aling cupcakes ang ginawa mo?**

   Answer: **Ginawa ko ang mga cupcakes na** _____.
   (far from both the speaker and the person being addressed.)

4. Question: **Sino ang kumain ng** _____?
   (close to the speaker)

   Answer: **Ako ang kumain ng apple pie na iyan.**

5. Question: **Sino ang kumain** _____?
   (far from the speaker)

   Answer: **Si Ralph ang kumain nito.**

DIALOGUE PRACTICE

Practice dialogues according to the following situations, using the sentences you have learned.

Situation 1 Your friend is visiting you at your home. You offer her a sandwich. However, she is full because she has eaten lunch.

YOU   : **Gusto mo ba ng** _____?

YOUR FRIEND : **Huwag na lang.** _____ **na ako.**

YOU   : **Sige na.**

YOUR FRIEND : **Kumain na ako ng** _____.

Situation 2 You and your brother are planning to have lunch together. He is asking you where and what you want to eat.

Your brother : **Saan mo gustong kumain?**

You : _____.

Your brother : **Ano ang gusto mong kainin?**

You : _____.

Situation 3 You are meeting a nutritionist. She wants to know what you eat for breakfast, lunch, and dinner.

Your nutritionist : **Ano ang kinakain mo sa almusal?**

You : _____.

Your nutritionist : **Ano ang kinakain mo sa tanghalian?**

You : _____.

Your nutritionist : **Ano ang kinakain mo sa hapunan?**

You : _____.

Situation 4 You are taking your friend out to dinner. You want to ask him/her what he/she would like to eat and drink so you can give the order to the waiter.

YOU   : _____?

YOUR FRIEND : **Gusto kong kumain ng spaghetti.**

YOU   : _____?

YOUR FRIEND : **Gusto kong uminom ng red wine.**

SUMMING UP

In this chapter, we learned words related to food and drink, as well as new expressions.

Write or talk about what you usually eat for breakfast, lunch, and dinner; the cutlery you use; and the food you like.

_____

_____

_____

_____

_____

_____

_____

_____

_____

_____

CHAPTER 9

Can I open a checking account?

Puwede po ba akong magbukas ng checking account?

In this chapter, we continue to learn about money and the directional focus of verbs. We will also practice honorifics or polite words such as **po/ho** and **opo/oho**, and we will review words which will help you describe yourself.

At the Bank

Melissa is at the bank because she wants to open a checking account.

magbukas	*to open*
gusto ko hong magbukas	*I want to open*
Gusto ko hong magbukas ng account.	Want + I + **ho** + **na** + open + **ng** + account. *I would like to open an account.*
klase	*kind*
Ano hong klaseng account?	What + **ho** + **na** + kind + **na** + account? *What kind of account?*
may dala	*bring*
pruweba	*proof*
pruweba ng tirahan	*proof of residence*
Nagdala ho ba kayo ng pruweba ng tirahan?	Brought + **ho** + **ba** + you + **ng** + proof of residence? *Did you bring proof of residence?*
kailangan	*should* (also means *need*)
sagutan	*fill out* (also means *answer*)
Kailangan niyo hong sagutan ang form na ito.	Should + you + **ho** + **na** + fill out + **ang** + form + **na** + this. *You need to fill out this form.*

 **DIALOGUE A**

MELISSA : **Gusto ko hong magbukas ng account.**
I would lke to open an account.
TELLER : **Ano hong klaseng account?** *What kind of account?*
MELISSA : **Checking account ho.** *A checking account.*
TELLER : **Nagdala ho ba kayo ng I.D. at pruweba ng tirahan?**
Did you bring an identification card and proof of residence?
MELISSA : **Heto ang pasaporte ko at ang electric bill ko.**
Here is my passport and my electric bill.
TELLER : **Kailangan niyo hong sagutin ang form na ito.**
You need to fill out this form.

VOCABULARY

Study the following additional words, phrases, and sentences.

buong pangalan	*complete name/full name*
apelyido	*last name*
Isulat mo ang pangalan mo.	*Write your name.*

pakisagutan	*please fill out*
Pakisagutan ang form.	*Please fill out the form.*
sagutin	*answer* (or *fill out*) (object focus)
tanong	*question*
Sagutin niyo ang mga tanong.	Answer + you + **ang** + questions. *Answer the questions.*

bukas	*open*
bintana	*window*
Bukas ang bintana.	Open + **ang** + window. *The window is open.*

> **VOCABULARY TIP (Spelling and meaning)** Some words which are spelled exactly the same may have different meanings. An example is the word **bukas**. When the accent is on the first syllable, it means *tomorrow*. When the accent is on the second syllable, it means *open*.

GRAMMAR AND PRACTICE

Let us continue our study of actor, object and directional focus by conjugating the verbs **bukas** (*open*), **dala** (*bring*), and **sagot** (*answer*). We will also study two new affixes, **i-** and **-an**.

Object Focus Using the Affix "i–"

In previous chapters, you have learned the use of affixes **mag-**, **-um-**, and **-in-**. Let us study another affix, **i-**, which like the affix **-in-**, is used when the focus is on the object of the sentence. In the same way that **mag-** and **-um-** are used with different verbs for the actor focus, **i-** and **-in-** are used with different verbs for the object focus. However, with **i-** verbs, both **i-** and **-in-** are used to form the completed aspect.

Here are the formulas for the use of the **i-** affix:

root word — bukas

infinitive/imperative form – **i-** + root word = **i-** + **bukas** = **ibukas**
completed aspect – **i-** + **-in-** before the first vowel of the root word + root word = **i-** + **-in-** before **u** + **bukas** = **ibinukas**
incompleted – first 3 syllable of completed form + root word = **ibinu** + **bukas** = **ibinubukas**
contemplated – **i-** + first syllable of root word + root word = **i-** + **bu** + **bukas** = **ibubukas**

Study the following verb charts.

Actor Focus: using the affixes "mag–" and "–um–"

Root	Inf/Imp	Completed	Incompleted	Contemplated
bukas	magbukas	nagbukas	nagbubukas	magbubukas
dala	magdala	nagdala	nagdadala	magdadala
sagot	sumagot	sumagot	sumasagot	sasagot

Object Focus: using the affixes "in–" and "i–"

Root	Inf/Imp	Completed	Incompleted	Contemplated
bukas	ibukas	ibinukas	ibinubukas	ibubukas
dala	dalhin	dinala	dinadala	dadalhin
sagot	sagutin	sinagot	sinasagot	isasagot/sasagutin

Directional Focus Using the Affixes "in-" and "-an"

Directional focus

If *who*-questions are answered by actor focus sentences, and *what*-questions are answered by object focus sentences, directional focus sentences respond to either *where*-questions or *for whom*-questions. Directional focus is used to give emphasis, and refers to the location, direction, or receiver of the action.

In the dialogue above, you learned the sentence below.

Kailangan niyo hong sagutan ang form na ito.　　*You need to fill out this form.*

This sentence responds to the following question.

Anong form ang kailangan kong sagutan?　　*What form do I need to fill out?*

To understand the difference between **in-** and **in- + -an** affixes, let us compare the following sentences. The focus of the sentence is in bold.

Actor Focus
Sumagot ako ng mga tanong sa form.　　*I answered the questions on the form.*

Object Focus
Sinagot ko ang mga tanong sa form.　　*The questions are what I answered on the form.*

Directional Focus (shows location of the questions)
Form ang sinagutan ko ng mga tanong.　　*It was on the form that I answered the questions.*

Here are other examples, this time showing the direction of the action.

Actor Focus
Nagdala ako ng identification card para sa bangko.　　*I brought an identification card for the bank.*

Object Focus
Identification card ang dinala ko para sa bangko.　　*An identification card is what I brought for the bank.*

Directional Focus (shows receiver of the action)

Bangko ang dinalhan ko ng identification card./ Dinalhan ko ng identification card ang bangko.	*It was for the bank that I brought the identification card.*

Study the following directional focus table.

Directional Focus Table: Using the affixes "in-" and "-an"

Root	Inf/Imp	Completed	Incompleted	Contemplated
bukas	buksan	binuksan	binubuksan	bubuksan
dala	dalhan	dinalhan	dinadalhan	dadalhan
sagot	sagutan	sinagutan	sinasagutan	sasagutan

Root Words and Verbs Review

Study how these root words and verbs are used in sentences.

May bukas na bintana.	*There is a window open.*
Gusto kong magbukas ng savings account.	*I want to open a savings account.*
Nagbukas ako ng savings account.	*I opened a savings account.*
Savings account ang binuksan ko.	*I opened a savings account.*
Nagdala akong pasaporte.	*I am bringing/I brought a passport.*
Nagdadala ako ng identification card sa library.	*I bring an identification card to the library (each time I go).*
Dinala ko ang libro para kay Melissa.	*I brought a book for Melissa.*
Dinalhan ko ng libro si Melissa.	*I brought a book for Melissa.* (Focus is on the direction of the action, "Melissa.")
Kailangan mong sagutan ang form.	*You need to fill out the form.*
Ako ang sasagot sa mga tanong sa form.	*I will fill out the form.*
Sasagutin ko ang mga tanong sa form.	*I will answer the questions on the form.*
Sasagutan ko ang form.	*I will fill out the form.* (Focus is on the direction of the action, "the form.")

DIALOGUE PRACTICE

Practice by asking and answering in the following situations.

Situation 1 You want to open a savings acount. You brought your passport. The teller asked you to fill out a form.

YOU	:	**Gusto ko hong _____ ng _____?**
TELLER	:	**Ano hong _____ account?**
YOU	:	_____.
TELLER	:	**May dala ho ba kayong _____?**
YOU	:	**Nagdala ho ako ng _____.**
TELLER	:	**Kailangan niyo hong _____ ang _____ na ito.**

Situation 2 You want to open a dollar account in Manila. You brought your identification card and proof of residence. After successfully opening an account, the bank manager asked you to fill out a performance survey form.

YOU	:	**Gusto _____.**
TELLER	:	**Ano ho ang _____ ninyong identification?**
YOU	:	_____.
BANK MANAGER	:	**Puwede niyo ho bang _____ ang performance survey na ito?**
YOU	:	_____.

Verifying Information

The teller is interviewing Melissa to verify the information on the form she has filled out. Study and review words you can use to talk about yourself.

nakatira	*living in* (referring to place of residence)
tirahan	*residence*
permanente	*permanent*
permanente niyong tirahan	*your permanent residence*
Ito ho ba ang permanente niyong tirahan?	This + **ho** + **ba** + **ang** + permanent + your + residence? *Is this your permanent residence?*

ay	used to mean *is/are* (particle)

Note: Ay cannot be translated into *is/are*, but it is used for the function of the verb *to be*. The particle **ay** is also called an inversion marker, which means it signals that the sentence is not using the common predicate-subject structure but the inverted structure subject-predicate.

Ang permanente ko pong tirahan ay 602 N. Westmoreland Avenue, Los Angeles, California.	**Ang** + permanant residence + I + **po** + **na** + residence + is + 602 N. Westmoreland Avenue, Los Angeles, California. *My permanent residence is 602 N. Westmoreland, Los Angeles, California.*
nagtatrabaho	*working*
estudyante	*student*
Estudyante po ako sa Unibersidad ng Pilipinas.	Student + **po** + I + at + University of the Philippines. *I am a student at the University of the Philippines.*

🔘 **DIALOGUE B**

TELLER : **Ano po ang buo ninyong pangalan?**
What is your complete name?

MELISSA : **Maria Luisa Roxas po ang buo kong pangalan.**
My complete name is Maria Luisa Roxas.

TELLER : **Saan ho kayo nakatira dito sa Metro Manila?**
Where do you live in Metro Manila?

MELISSA : **Nakatira ho ako sa 32 Masaya Street, UP Village, Quezon City.** *I live at 32 Masaya Street, UP Village, Quezon City.*

TELLER : **Ito ho ba ang permanente ninyong tirahan?**
Is this your permanent address?

MELISSA : **Hindi po. Ang permanente ko pong tirahan ay 602 N Westmoreland Avenue, Los Angeles, California.**
No. My permanent address is 602 N. Westmoreland Avenue, Los Angeles, California.

TELLER : **Nagtatrabaho po ba kayo?** *Do you work?*

MELISSA : **Hindi po. Estudyante po ako sa Unibersidad ng Pilipinas.**
No. I am a student at the University of the Philippines.

> **VOCABULARY TIP (English Words)** Many English words have been integrated
> into the Tagalog language. One such word is "address," which is sometimes giv-
> en the Tagalog spelling **adres**, or is translated into **tirahan** (residence). **Tirahan**
> refers only to a residential address and not a business address.

QUESTION AND ANSWER PRACTICE

Describe yourself by answering the following questions.

1. Question: **Ano ang buo ninyong pangalan?**

   Answer: _____ ang _____ kong pangalan.

2. Question: **Saan kayo nakatira?**

   Answer: _____ ako sa _____.

3. Question: **Pakisulat ho ang permanente ninyong tirahan.**

   Answer: **Ang** _____ **kong adres ay**

   _____.

4. Question: **Estudyante ba kayo o nagtatrabaho na?**

   Answer: _____ **ako.**

5. Question: **Saan ho kayo** _____?

   Answer: _____ **ako sa** _____.

SUMMING UP

Practice what you have learned in Chapter 9. Talk or write about a bank account you have opened, the kind of account, and where you opened it. Also talk about your current and permanent addresses.

_____

_____

_____

_____

_____

_____

_____

_____

_____

_____

CHAPTER 10

What is the exchange rate?
Magkano ang palitan ng pera?

In this chapter, we'll learn about money, and how to use the polite affix **paki-**. We will also practice numbers, and study helping verbs and the infinitive form of the verb.

At the money exchange counter

Ralph is at a money exchange counter. He wants to know what the exchange rate is.

Here are a few words, phrases, and sentences related to money:

palitan	*exchange rate*
dolyar	*dollars*
ngayon	*today; now*
ho	honorific word (used to show respect)
Ano ho ang palitan sa dolyar ngayon?	What + **ho** + **ang** + exchange rate + in + dollar + now? *What is the exchange rate for dollars today?*
kuwarenta	*forty* (Spanish-derived)
kwarenta'y dos	*forty two* (Spanish-derived)
apatnapu't dalawa	*forty two* (indigenous Tagalog)
piso	*pesos* (indigenous Tagalog)
pesos	*pesos* (Spanish-derived)
sentimos	*cents*
singkuwenta sentimos	*fifty cents*
at	*and*
Kuwarenta'y dos pesos at singkuwenta sentimos sa isang dolyar.	Forty two pesos + fifty cents + to + one + dollar. *Forty two pesos and fifty cents to the dollar.*
magkano	*how much*
ang gusto niyo	*you want*
palit	*exchange* (root word)

papalitan	*exchange* (verb, directional focus)
gusto niyong papalitan	*want to exchange*
Magkano ho ang gusto niyong papalitan?	How much + **ho** + **ang** + want you + **na** + exchange? *How much do you want to exchange?*
magpa-	affix (means *to have someone do something*)
magpapalit	*have someone exchange* (actor focus)
Puwede ho ba akong magpapalit ng dalawang daang dolyar?	Can + **ho** + **ba** + I + **na** + have exchanged + **ng** + two hundred dollars? *Can I exchange two hundred dollars?*
kita	*see* (root word)
makita	*to see*
Puwede ko ho bang makita ang I.D. ninyo?	Can + I + **ho** + **ba** + **na** + see + **ang** + I.D. + your? *Can I see your identification card?*
Heto ho.	Here + **ho**. *Here you are.*
walong libo at limang daang piso	*eight thousand and five hundred pesos*
Heto ho ang walong libo at limang daang piso.	Here + **ho** + **ang** + eight thousand + and + five hundred + pesos. *Here is eight thousand and four hundred pesos.*
paki-	*please* (affix)
bilang	*count* (verb); *number* (noun)
pakibilang	*please count*
Pakibilang po ninyo.	Please count + **po** + you. *Please count it.*

DIALOGUE A

RALPH : **Magandang hapon ho.** *Good afternoon.*
CLERK : **Magandang hapon naman.** *Good afternoon too.*
RALPH : **Ano ho ang palitan sa dolyar ngayon?** *What is the exchange rate for dollars today?*
CLERK : **Kuwarenta'y dos pesos at singkuwenta sentimos sa isang dolyar. Magkano ho ang gusto niyong papalitan?**
Forty-two pesos to the dollar. How much do you want to exchange?
RALPH : **Puwede ho ba akong magpapalit ng dalawang daang dolyar?**
Can I exchange two hundred dollars?

CLERK : **Oho. Puwede ko ho bang makita ang I.D. ninyo?**
Can I see your identification card?

RALPH : **Heto ho.** *Here you are.*

CLERK : **Heto ho ang walong libo at limang daang piso. Pakibilang po ninyo.** *Here is eight thousand and four hundred pesos. Please count it.*

CULTURE TIP (Exchanging Money) In the Philippines, there are money exchange stalls or small shops all around the cities. Filipinos go to these stalls or shops more often than to the banks because they are perceived to have better exchange rates. Alternatively, you can also exchange money at designated counters in shopping malls.

GRAMMAR AND PRACTICE

By now, you are familiar with the affixes **mag-**, **-um-**, and **-in-**, and two kinds of focuses, actor and object. Let us study some new affixes, **paki-**, **magpa-**, and **pina-**, and a new focus, the directional focus.

1. The affix "paki-"
The affix **paki-** means "please," and is used in the same way as **pa** (also meaning "please"), which you learned in Chapter 7.

Here are some words and sentences using **paki-**.

Pakibilang ang mga libro mo.	*Please count your books.*
Pakibigay sa akin ang papel ko.	*Please give me my paper.*
Pakikain ang almusal mo.	*Please eat your breakfast.*

2. "Magpapalit," and the affixes "magpa-," "pina-" with "-an"
Magpapalit literally means "to ask someone to change for you." However, in contemporary times, it has also come to mean "to change money." Similarly when one talks about "exchange rate," one simply asks: **Ano ang palitan?** (Literally, *What is the exchange?*)

The verb **magpapalit** uses the affix **magpa-**, which means "to cause an action." Let us study the sentence, **Nagpapalit si Ralph ng dollars sa Manila Money Exchange Center.** (*Ralph changed dollars at the Manila Money Exchange Center.*) The focus of the sentence is Ralph as indicated by the marker **si**, and Ralph is called the causer of the action.

If we want to keep the idea that Ralph causes the action, but change the focus to the direction of the action, we would use the affix **pina-** with -an, and say "**Pinapalitan ni Ralph ang dollars niya sa Manila Money Exchange Center.**" (*Dollars are what Ralph changed at the Manila Money Exchange Center.*)

To summarize, the affix **magpa-** is used when the focus is on the causer of the action, while **pina-** with -an is used when the focus is on the direction of the action.

Compare the following sentences with verbs using the root word **gawa** (*make*). The first sentence uses the affix -**um**-, and focuses on the actor, "my sister." The second sentence uses the affix -**in**-, and focuses on the object, "the cake." The last two sentences use the affixes **magpa-** ("I", the causer of the action, is the focus) and **pina-** (the person performing the action is the focus).

Gumawa ng cake ang kapatid ko.	*My sister made a cake.*
Cake ang ginawa ng kapatid ko.	*A cake is what my sister made.*
Nagpagawa ako ng cake sa kapatid ko.	*I asked my sister to make a cake.*
Pinagawa ko ng cake ang kapatid ko.	*My sister is whom I asked to make a cake.*

Again, the marker **ang** (and for proper nouns, **si**) provides us with clues on the focus of the sentence. In the third sentence, the subject pronoun **ako** (instead of the object pronoun **ko**), also tells us that that the causer of the action is the focus.

3. Conjugating "magpapalit"

Let us see how **magpapalit** can be used. Study the chart below, the first row shows actor focus, and the second, directional focus.

Root	Infinitive	Completed	Incompleted	Contemplated
palit (actor focus)	magpapalit	nagpapalit	nagpapapalit	magpapapalit
palit (directional focus)	papalitan	pinapalitan	pinapapalitan	papapalitan

Now, what were the formulas used to conjugate the above verbs?

Actor focus formulas:

Infinitive – **magpa** + root word = **magpa** + **palit** = **magpapalit**
Completed – **nagpa** + root word = **nagpa** + **palit** = **nagpapalit**
Incompleted – **nagpa** + **pa** + root word = **nagpa** + **pa** + **palit** = **nagpa-papalit**
Contemplated – change **n** in incompleted form to **m** = **magpapapalit**

Directional focus (for causative verbs) formulas

Infinitive – **pa** + root word + **an** = **pa** + **palit** + **an** = **papalitan**
Completed – **pina** + root word + **an** = **pina** + **palit** + **an** = **pinapalitan**
Incompleted – **pina** + **pa** + root word + **an** = **pina** + **pa** + **palit** + **an** = **pinapapalitan**
Contemplated – **pa** + first syllable of root word + root word + **an** = **pa** + **pa** + **palit** + **an** = **papapalitan**

Study how the verb forms above can be used in sentences.

1. Question: **Saan ka nagpapalit ng pera?**
   Where did you exchange money?

   Answer: **Nagpapalit ako ng pera sa Manila Money Exchange Center.** *I exchanged money at the Manila Money Exchange Center.*

2. Question: **Magkano ang pinapalitan mo?**
   How much did you exchange?

   Answer 1: **Nagpapalit ako ng dalawang daang dolyar.**
   I exchanged two hundred dollars.

   Answer 2: **Dalawang daang dolyar ang pinapalitan ko.**
   I exchanged two hundred dollars.

3. Question: **Magkano ang gusto mong papalitan?**
   How much would you like to exchange?

   Answer: **Gusto kong magpapalit ng isang daang libong yen.**
   I would like to exchange one hundred thousand yen.

4. Question: **Saan ako puwedeng magpapalit ng euro?**
   Where can I exchange euros?

   Answer: **Puwede kang magpapalit ng euro sa Manila Bank.**
   You can exchange euros at Manila Bank.

> **VOCABULARY TIP (Counting Money)** When we count money using indigenous Tagalog numbers, we use the word **piso**. When we count using Spanish-derived numbers, we use **pesos**. For example, for "forty pesos," we can say **apatnapung piso** or **kuwarenta pesos**, respectively.

DIALOGUE PRACTICE

Create dialogues for the following situations.

Situation 1 You are at a money exchange counter. You want to know the exchange rate between euros and Philippine pesos. You want to exchange 100 euros.

You : **Gusto ko hong _____.**
Clerk : **Magkano ang gusto mong papalitan?**
You : **_____ euro. Ano ho ang _____?**
Clerk : **51.72 pesos sa isang euro.**
You : **Heto ho ang _____ euro.**
Clerk : **Heto ho ang _____ piso.**

Situation 2 You just came from Makati Money Exchange. Your friend asked you where you had your money exchanged, and what the exchange rate was.

Your Friend : **Saan ka nagpapalit ng pera?**
You : _____.
Your Friend : **Magkano ang pinapalitan mo?**
You : _____.
Your Friend : **Ano ang palitan ngayon?**
You : _____.

Situation 3 You plan to exchange two hundred Australian dollars into Philippine pesos. However, the nearest money exchange counter to your hotel does not exchange Australian dollars. You want to ask the hotel clerk where you can go.

You : _____?
Hotel Clerk : **Puwede ho kayong magpapalit ng Australian dollars sa Manila Bank.**
You : _____?

HOTEL CLERK : **45.34 po ang palitan. Magkano ho ang gusto ninyong papalitan?**

YOU   : _____

_____?

The Best Rates

Melissa is calling up Ralph to ask about exchange rates. She is going to Japan and would like to change her pesos into yen. In the earlier dialogue, you learned how to talk about exchange rates. In this dialogue, learn how to compare exchange rates.

nga	used for emphasis
Si Ralph nga ito.	*This is Ralph.*
mataas ang palitan	*the exchange rate is high*
mas mataas ang palitan	*the exchange rate is higher*
Saan mas mataas ang palitan?	Where + higher + **ang** + exchange rate? *Where is the exchange rate higher?*
Mas mataas sa Manila Money Exchange.	Higher + at + Manila Money Exchange. *It is higher at Manila Money Exchange.*
pero	*but*
mas malapit	*nearer; closer*
Mas mataas sa Manila Money Exchange pero mas malapit ka sa Cubao Money Exchange.	Higher + at + Manila Money Exchange + but + closer + you + at + Cubao Money Exchange. *It is higher at Manila Money Exchange but you are closer to Cubao Money Exchange.*
kaya	*what about* (also used to mean *because*)
Sa Makati Money Exchange kaya?	At + Makati Money Exchange + what about? *What about Makati Money Exchange?*
pinakamababa	*lowest*
Pinakamababa ang exchange rate doon.	Lowest + **ang** + exchange rate + there. *The exchange rate is lowest there.*

 **DIALOGUE B**

MELISSA : **Hello, Ralph?** *Hello, Ralph?*

RALPH : **Oo, si Ralph nga ito.** *Yes, this is Ralph.*

MELISSA : **Si Melissa ito. Gusto kong magpapalit ng pera. Saan mas mataas ang palitan?** *This is Melissa. I want to exchange money. Where is the exchange rate higher? [= where can I get better rates?]*

RALPH : **Mas mataas sa Manila Money Exchange, pero mas malapit ka sa Cubao Money Exchange.** *It is higher at Manila Money Exchange, but you are closer to Cubao Money Exchange.*

MELISSA : **Sa Makati Money Exchange kaya?** *What about in Makati Money Exchange?*

RALPH : **Pinakamababa ang exchange rate doon.** *The exchange rate is lowest there.*

VOCABULARY AND GRAMMAR

Practice comparatives and superlatives by studying the following words and phrases.

pinakamataas ang palitan	*the exchange rate is highest*
mababa	*low*
mas mababa	*lower*
pinakamababa	*lowest*
malapit	*near/close*
mas malapit	*nearer/closer*
pinakamalapit	*nearest/closest*
malayo	*far*
mas malayo	*farther away*
pinakamalayo	*farthest*

For comparatives, simply add **mas** before the word. For example, **mataas** (*high*) becomes **mas mataas** (*higher*).

For superlatives, simply add the affix **pinaka-** before the root word. Thus, **mataas** (*high*) becomes **pinakamataas** (*the highest*).

QUESTION AND ANSWER PRACTICE

Practice comparatives and superlatives by asking and answering questions.

1. Question: **Ano ang pinakamalapit na bangko sa bahay mo?**

   Answer: **Pinakamalapit ang _____ sa bahay ko.**

2. Question: **Alin ang mas malapit sa bahay mo, ang bangko o ang money exchange center?**

   Answer: _____.

3. Question: **Alin ang mas mataas ngayon, ang yen o ang dolyar?**

   Answer: _____.

4. Question: _____?

   Answer: **Pinakamalayo ang Makati Money Exchange sa bahay ni Melissa.**

SUMMING UP

Let us review what you have just learned in Chapter 10. Talk or write about the last time you exchanged money, where you exchanged it, and what the exchange rate was.

_____

_____

_____

_____

_____

_____

_____

_____

_____

_____

CHAPTER 11

What time is it?
Anong oras na?

In this chapter, we'll learn about the two ways of telling time in Tagalog: the indigenous way and the Spanish-derived way. You will also learn how to talk about your activities before going to bed and after waking up.

Waking Up

Sarah is eating breakfast at the dining table. Melissa has just woke up and she doesn't have time to eat because she needs to be at the university by 8:00 a.m.

Here are a few words, phrases, and sentences you need to learn before reading the dialogues.

oras	*time*
anong oras	*what time*
gising	*wake up* (root word)
gumising	*woke up*
Anong oras ka gumising?	What + **na** + time + you + woke up? *What time did you wake up?*
ala-sais ng umaga/ ika-anim ng umaga	*6:00 a.m.*
alas-siyete ng umaga/ ika-pito ng umaga	*7:00 a.m.*
alas-otso ng umaga/ ika-walo ng umaga	*8:00 a.m.*
Alas-siyete na ng umaga.	Seven o'clock + already + in + morning. *It is seven o'clock.*
muna	*first; beforehand; doing something before doing something else*
upo	*sit* (root word)
umupo	*sit* (imperative form)
kain	*eat* (root word)

kumain	*eat* (imperative form)
at	*and*
Umupo ka muna at kumain.	Sit + you + first + and + eat. *Sit down and eat.*
naku	*Oh!* or *Oh no!* (interjection)
Naku, wala akong oras.	Oh no + don't have + I + **na** + time *Oh no, I don't have time.*
tulog	*sleep* (root word)
natulog	*slept*
kagabi	*last night*
Anong oras ka natulog kagabi?	What + **na** + time + you + slept last night? *What time did you sleep last night?*
nang	*at* (used as a preposition in this chapter to introduce an adverbial phrase; can also be used as an adverb to mean *when*)
ng	used here to mean *of*
ng gabi	*in the evening*
Natulog ako nang alas-diyes ng gabi.	Slept + I + at + ten o'clock+ of + evening. *I slept at 10 o'clock in the evening.*
bakit	*why*
walang oras	*no time*
Bakit wala kang oras?	Why + don't have + you + **na** + time? *Why don't you have the time?*
klase	*class*
Alas-otso ang klase ko.	Eight o'clock + **ang** + class + my. *My class is at eight o'clock.*
na	*already*
ba	used here for emphasis (also used for Yes/No questions)
Anong oras na ba?	What + **na** + time + already + **ba**? *What time is it?*

SARAH : **Magandang umaga, Melissa.** *Good morning, Melissa.*

MELISSA : **Magandang umaga naman, Sarah. Anong oras ka gumising?** *Good morning, Sarah. What time did you wake up?*

SARAH : **Alas-sais.** *6 o'clock.*

MELISSA : **Anong oras ka natulog kagabi?** *What time did you sleep last night?*

SARAH : **Natulog ako nang alas-diyes ng gabi. Umupo ka muna at kumain.** *I slept at 10 o'clock in the evening. Sit down and eat.*

MELISSA : **Anong oras na ba?** *What time is it (now)?*

SARAH : **Alas-siyete na ng umaga.** *It is 7 o'clock.*

MELISSA : **Naku, wala akong oras.** *Oh no, I don't have time.*

SARAH : **Bakit wala kang oras?** *Why don't you have the time?*

MELISSA : **Alas-otso ang klase ko.** *My class is at 8 o'clock.*

VOCABULARY

Study the following ways of expressing time.

SPANISH–DERIVED	TAGALOG	
ala-una	ika-isa	*one o'clock*
alas-dos	ikalawa	*two o'clock*
alas-tres	ikatlo	*three o'clock*
alas-kuwatro	ika-apat	*four o'clock*
alas-singko	ikalima	*five o'clock*
alas-sais	ika-anim	*six o'clock*
alas-siyete	ikapito	*seven o'clock*
alas-otso	ikawalo	*eight o'clock*
alas-nuwebe	ikasiyam	*nine o'clock*
alas-diyes	ikasampu	*ten o'clock*
alas-onse	ikalabing-isa	*eleven o'clock*
alas-dose	ikalabindalawa	*twelve o'clock*
oras		*time; hour*
minuto		*minute*
segundo		*second*
ng umaga		*in the morning*
ng tanghali		*at noon*

ng hapon		*in the afternoon*
ng gabi		*in the evening*
madaling-araw		*dawn*
tanghali		*noon*
tanghaling tapat		*exactly at noon*
hatinggabi		*midnight*
makalipas		*after*
relo		*watch*
orasan		*clock*
y medya	**kalahati**	*half* (used for thirty minutes)
menos ... para	**bago ang**	*before*
maaga		*early*

The word pairs **menos ... para** and **bago ang** are used for indicating minutes before reaching an hour. For example:

<u>menos </u>singko <u>para</u> alas-onse	*five minutes before eleven*
limang minuto <u>bago ang</u> ikalabing-isa	*five minutes before eleven*

Here are some examples of ways to tell the time.

Alas-kuwatro na ng hapon.	*It is four o'clock in the afternoon.*
Ika-apat na ng hapon.	*It is four o'clock in the afternoon.*
Alas-tres kuwarenta y singko na.	*It is three forty-five.*
Labinlimang minuto na lang bago ang alas-kuwatro.	*It is just fifteen minutes before four.*
Alas-kuwatro kinse na ng hapon.	*It is four fifteen in the afternoon.*
Labinlimang minuto na makalipas ang alas-kuwatro.	*It is fifteen minutes after four.*
Tanghaling tapat na.	*It is exactly noon.*
Hatinggabi na.	*It is exactly midnight.*

Here are examples of sentences which you can use to talk about sleeping and waking up. Note that time is not exact in Filipino culture. For example, when you wake up late, you can use the word **tanghali** (*noon*) when in fact, you woke up at around 10 a.m. and you just want to say you woke up late.

Gumising ako nang maaga.	*I woke up early.*

Natulog ako nang maaga.	*I slept early.*
Tanghali na ako gumising.	*I woke up at noon./I woke up late.* (literally, It was late already when I woke up.)
Gabi na ako natulog.	*I slept late.* (literally, It was late already when I slept.)

CULTURE TIP (Filipino Time) Filipinos always use the phrase "Filipino time." This refers to the flexibility of time among Filipinos. For example, "seven o'clock" can mean anytime from six to eight o'clock. Flexibility is true for many aspects of Filipino culture—from the meaning of words, to time, to relationships.

GRAMMAR AND PRACTICE:

Using "nang" and "ng"

The use of **nang** and **ng** (also pronounced **nang**) comes into focus in sentences that have adverbial phrases or phrases that describe the action.

In the dialogue above, you learned a sentence that uses both the long **nang** and the short **ng**.

Natulog ako **nang** alas-diyes **ng** gabi. *I slept at 10 o'clock in the evening.*

The adverbial phrase **alas-diyes ng gabi** (*10 o'clock in the evening*) describes the action **natulog** (*slept*).

Similarly, we can say the following sentences using adverbs such as **maaga** (*early*). In these examples, **maaga** (*early*) describes the actions **gumising** (*woke up*) and **natulog** (*slept*).

Gumising si Sarah nang maaga.	*Sarah woke up early.*
Natulog si Sarah nang maaga.	*Sarah slept early.*

When do we use the short **ng**? In previous lessons, you have learned the use of **ng** as an object marker when the focus of sentence is on the actor or doer of the action. In the examples below, **ng** marks the object (the sandwich).

Gumawa si Sarah ng sandwich.	*Sarah made a sandwich.*
Kumain si Sarah ng sandwich.	*Sarah ate a sandwich.*

For this chapter, we are studying the use of **ng** as a preposition. Study the use of **ng** in the phrase below.

alas diyes <u>ng</u> gabi   *ten o'clock in the evening*
                       (literally, ten o'clock of evening)

In the English translation, **ng** is translated into *in*. However, grammarians such as Schacter and Otanes, explain that **ng** is actually closer to in this phrase.

To avoid confusion, remember two things.

1. Use **ng** when followed by a noun.
2. Use **nang** when followed by an adverb or an adverbial phrase.

The affix "na–" for actor focus sentences

In previous lessons, you have learned two affixes **mag-** and **um-**, both of which are used when the focus is on the actor or doer of the action.

In this chapter, we are studying the third affix for actor focus sentences. You learned the following sentences in the dialogue.

Anong oras ka natulog kagabi?   *What time did you sleep last* night?
Natulog ako nang alas-diyes   *I slept at 10 o'clock last night.*
  ng gabi.

Natulog (*slept*) uses the affix **na-**. Na- is a variation of the affix **ma-**, and both are used often, but not all the time, in instances when an action is done involuntarily or accidentally. To conjugate verbs using the affix **na-/ma-** we can use the following formulas:

root word – tulog

infinitive/imperative form – **ma-** + root word = **ma** + **tulog** = **matulog**
completed aspect – **na** + root word = **na** + **tulog** = **natulog**
incompleted – first two syllables of completed aspect + root word = **natu**
  + **tulog** = **natutulog**
contemplated – change the **n** in the incompleted aspect to **m** = **natutulog**
  minus **n** + **m** = **matutulog**

Conjugation Practice

For this chapter, let us practice four verbs: **gumising** (*woke up*), **bumangon** (*got up*), **umupo** (*sat*), and **natulog** (*slept*). These verbs do not take objects, so we will just concentrate on actor focus. Note the use of the -**um-** and na- affixes.

Root	Inf/Imp	Completed	Incomplete	Contemplated
gising	gumising	gumising	gumigising	gigising
bangon	bumangon	bumangon	bumabangon	babangon
upo	umupo	umupo	umuupo	uupo
tulog	matulog	natulog	natutulog	matutulog

Study the following sentences.

Gusto kong gumising nang alas-sais ng umaga.	*I want to wake up at six o'clock in the morning.*
Gumising ako nang alas-siyete ng umaga.	*I woke up at six o'clock in the morning.*
Gumigising ako nang alas-sais ng umaga.	*I wake up at six o'clock in the morning.*
Gigising ako nang alas-sais ng umaga.	*I will wake up at six o'clock in the morning.*

Complete the following sentences. Write down the time indicated by the numerals.

Gusto kong bumangon nang (7:00) _____ ng umaga.

_____ ako ng (7:30) _____ ng umaga.

_____ ako ng (7:15) _____ ng umaga.

_____ ako ng (7:10) _____ ng umaga.

Gusto kong matulog nang (10:00) _____ ng gabi

_____ ako ng (11:00) _____ ng gabi.

_____ ng (10:30) _____ ng gabi.

_____ ako ng (10:15) _____ ng gabi.

Time Practice

Write the time in both the indigenous way and the Spanish-derived way.

	Indigenous	Spanish-derived
3:15 p.m.:	_____	_____
9:30 a.m.:	_____	_____
11:25 p.m.:	_____	_____

5:20 a.m.: _____   _____

6:45 p.m.: _____   _____

QUESTION AND ANSWER PRACTICE

Talk about your daily schedule.

Question: **Anong oras ka natutulog?**

Answer: _____ **ako nang** _____.

Question: **Anong** _____ **ka gumigising?**

Answer: _____ **ako nang** _____.

Question: _____**ka bumabangon?**

Answer: _____ **nang** _____.

Evening Activities

Sarah and Melissa are eating dinner in their apartment.

mag-aaral	*will study*
pagkatapos	*after*
pagkatapos kumain	*after eating*
pa	*still; also*
Mag-aaral ka pa ba pagkatapos kumain?	Will study + you + still + after + eating? *Will you study after eating?*
nag-aral na ako	studied + already + I. *I studied*
pagkatapos ng klase ko	*after my class*
Nag-aral na ako pagkatapos ng klase ko.	Studied + already + I + after + class + my. *I studied after my class.*
gawa	*do* (root word)
gagawin	*will do*
Ano ang gagawin mo?	What + **ang** + will do + you? *What will you do?*
praktis/ensayo	*practice* (root word)
magpapraktis/mag-eensayo	*will practice*
bago matulog	*before sleeping*
Magpapraktis ako ng flute bago matulog.	Practice + I + **ng** + flute + before + sleeping. *I will practice the flute before sleeping.*

basa (accent on the first syllable)	*read* (root word)
magbabasa	*will read*
bago maligo	*before taking a bath*
Magbabasa ako ng libro bago maligo.	Will read + I + **ng** + book + before + taking a bath. *I will read before taking a bath.*

 DIALOGUE B

SARAH : **Mag-aaral ka pa ba pagkatapos kumain?**
Will you study after eating?

MELISSA : **Hindi. Nag-aral na ako pagkatapos ng klase ko.**
No. I studied after my class.

SARAH : **Ano ang gagawin mo?** *What will you do?*

MELISSA : **Magpapraktis ako ng flute bago matulog. Ikaw?**
I will practice the flute before going to sleep. And you?

SARAH : **Magbabasa ako ng libro bago maligo.**
I will read a book before taking a bath.

VOCABULARY AND GRAMMAR

Let us study new verbs that express daily activities using the actor and object focuses. Additionally, let us study the use of the words **bago** (*before*) and **pagkatapos** (*after*).

laro	*play* (a game) (root word)
maglalaro	*will play* (a game)
tugtog	*play* (a musical instrument) (root word)
tutugtog	*will play* (a musical instrument)
maglalaro ng computer game na Bejewelled	*will play the computer game* called Bejewelled
tutugtog ng gitara	*will play the guitar*
nood	*watch* (root word)
manonood ng telebisyon	*will watch television*
manonood ng palabas sa telebisyon	*will watch a show on television*
kinig	*listen* (root word)
makikinig ng musika	*will listen to music*

Now, let us conjugate these verbs using the actor focus.

Actor Focus

Root	Inf/Imp	Completed	Incompleted	Comtemplated
laro	maglaro	naglaro	naglalaro	maglalaro
tugtog	tumugtog	tumugtog	tumutugtog	tutugtog
nood	manood	nanood	nanonood	manonood
kinig	makinig	nakinig	nakikinig	makikinig

Verbs with "bago" (before) and "pagkatapos" (after)

Study the following sentences that use **bago** (*before*) and **pagkatapos** (*after*). Remember that the verb that follows the words **bago** and **pagkatapos** should use the infinitive/imperative form.

Maglalaro ako ng Bejewelled na computer game pagkatapos kumain.
  I will play the computer game Bejewelled *after eating.*
Tutugtog ako ng piano bago matulog. *I will play the piano before sleeping.*
Manonood ako ng soap opera sa telebisyon pagkatapos kumain. *I will watch a soap opera on television after eating.*
Makikinig ako ng musikang klasikal pagkatapos matulog. *I will listen to classical music before sleeping.*

Object Focus

Now practice the use of the same verbs using object focus. Note the verb **laro**, which is an irregular verb. Instead of conjugating **laro** into **linaro** (completed) and **linalaro** (incompleted), we use **nilaro** (completed) and **nilalaro** (incompleted).

Root	Inf/Imp	Completed	Incompleted	Comtemplated
laro	laruin	nilaro	nilalaro	lalaruin
tugtog	tugtugin	tinugtog	tinutugtog	tutugtugin
nood	panoorin	pinanood	pinanonood	panonoorin
kinig	pakinggan	pinakinggan	pinakikinggan	pakikinggan

Now, let us compare the object focus to the actor focus. The four sentences below have the exact meaning as the sentences earlier, but now the focus is on the object.

Bejewelled na computer game ang lalaruin ko pagkatapos kumain.
  Bejewelled *is the computer game I will play after eating.*
Piano ang tutugtugin ko bago matulog. *The piano is what I will play before sleeping.*

Soap opera sa telebisyon ang panonoorin ko pagkatapos kumain. *A soap opera on television is what I will watch after eating.*
Musikang klasikal ang pakikinggan ko bago matulog. *Classical music is what I will listen to before sleeping.*

As explained in a previous chapter, sentences using the object focus are best understood as responses to **ano** (*what*) questions. For example:

Anong computer game ang lalaruin mo bago kumain? *What computer game are you playing before eating?*
Anong instrumento ang tutugtugin mo bago matulog? *What instrument are you playing before sleeping?*
Anong palabas ang panonoorin mo sa telebisyon pagkatapos kumain? *What will you watch on television after eating?*

DIALOGUE PRACTICE

1. Pretend you are talking to a friend. He/she is asking you what time you went to bed last night, what time you woke up, and what you did before and after. You watched a game show on television before going to bed, and ate breakfast after you woke up.

YOUR FRIEND : **Anong oras ka natulog?**

YOU : _____ ako nang _____ ng gabi.

YOUR FRIEND : **Ano ang ginawa mo bago ka natulog?**

YOU : _____ ako ng _____ sa telebisyon
bago ako _____.

YOUR FRIEND : **Anong _____ ka gumising?**

YOU : _____ng umaga.

YOUR FRIEND : **Ano ang _____ mo pagkatapos mong _____?**

YOU : _____ ako ng almusal pagkatapos _____.

> **GRAMMAR TIP (Tenses And Aspects)** Always remember that there are no tenses in Tagalog, only aspects. Please don't be confused if the English equivalent of a Tagalog verb is not what you may expect.

SUMMING UP

Practice telling the time. Look at your watch. What is the time now? What time will you do your next activity? What time is your first appointment tomorrow? What time will you be home tomorrow?

CHAPTER 12

What time do you eat breakfast?
Anong oras ka nag–aalmusal?

In this chapter, you will learn words that you can use to describe your everyday activities, adverbs of frequency, and verbs that express habitual action.

An Invitation

It is Saturday morning and Ralph is having breakfast at home. He receives a call from his colleague and friend, Mr. Richard Tolentino.

Mabuti naman.	*It's good!* (can also mean *fine*).
Gising ka na.	Awake + you + already. *You're awake.*
Mabuti naman at gising ka na.	Good + awake + you + already. *Great, you're up!*
nag-eehersisyo	*exercises* (referring to physical exercise)
tuwing	*every*
Nag-eehersisyo ako tuwing alas-siyete ng umaga.	Exercise + I + every + seven o'clock + of + morning. *I exercise at seven o'clock in the morning.*
almusal	*breakfast*
Kumakain na ako ng almusal.	Eating + already + I + **ng** + breakfast. *I am eating breakfast.*
tawag	*call* (root word)
tumawag	*called*
dahil	*because*
tumawag ako dahil	called + I + because *I called because*
maggo-golf	*will play golf*
maggo-golf kami ng mga kaibigan ko	will play golf + we + **ng** + friends + my *my friends and I will play golf*

Tumawag ako dahil maggo-golf kami ng mga kaibigan ko.	Called + I + because + will play golf + we + **ng** + friends + my. *I called because my friends and I are playing golf.*
sama	*go with; join* (root word)
sumama	*go with; join*
Gusto mo bang sumama sa amin?	Want + you + **ba** + **na** + join + to + us? *Would you like to join us?*
daan	*pass by; pick up*
dadaanan	*will pass by; will pick up someone*
nang	*at* (also used as a relative pronoun)
Dadaanan ka namin nang alas-otso.	Will pick up + you + we + at + eight o'clock. *We will pick you up at eight o'clock.*

 **DIALOGUE A**

RALPH : **Hello? Magandang umaga.** *Hello? Good morning.*

RICHARD : **Hello? Magandang umaga rin. Si Ralph ba ito?**
Hello. Good morning too. Is this Ralph?

RALPH : **Oo, si Ralph nga ito.** *Yes, this is Ralph.*

RICHARD : **Ralph! Mabuti naman at gising ka na.** *Ralph! Great, you're up!*

RALPH : **Oo, nag-eehersisyo ako tuwing alas-siyete ng umaga. Kumakain na ako ng almusal.** *Yes, I exercise at seven o'clock in the morning. I am eating breakfast.*

RICHARD : **Tumawag ako dahil maggo-golf kami sa Tagaytay ng mga kaibigan ko. Gusto mo bang sumama sa amin?**
I called because my friends and I are playing golf in Tagaytay. Would you like to join us?

RALPH : **Anong oras?** *What time?*

RICHARD : **Dadaanan ka namin nang alas-otso.** *We will pick you up at eight o'clock.*

VOCABULARY

Here are some words you can use when talking about your day. The root words appear in parenthesis beside the verbs. Also remember to review some of the words you have learned in previous chapters, such as the incompleted form of the verbs **gumigising** (**gising**; *wake up*), **nag-aaral** (**aral**; *study*), **nagtatrabaho** (**trabaho**; *work*), **naglalaro** (**laro**; *play [a* *game]*), **tumutugtog** (tugtog; *play [an instrument]*), **nakikinig** (root word kinig; *listen*), **nanonood** (nood; *watch*) and **natutulog** (tulog; *sleep*).

naghihilamos (hilamos)	*wash one's face*
naliligo/nagsa-shower (ligo/shower)	*take a bath/shower*
nagsesepilyo (sepilyo)	*brush teeth*
nagbibihis (bihis)	*dress up*
pumapasok (pasok)	*go to* (class/work)
nagluluto (luto)	*cook*
naglilinis (linis)	*clean*
namamasyal (pasyal)	*go around*
namimili (bili)	*shop*
naglalakad (lakad)	*walk*
tumatakbo (takbo)	*run*
sumasayaw (sayaw)	*dance*
kumakanta (kanta)	*sing*
nagbabasa (basa)	*read*
nag-eensayo (ensayo)	*practice* (for example, practice a musical instrument or a sport)
umuuwi (uwi)	*go home*
mula	*from*
hanggang	*to/until*
mula alas-otso y medya hanggang alas-singko	*from eight-thirty to five o'clock*

You may also want to use words derived from English. Simply use the incompleted form of the verb, who is **nag-** + the first syllable of the root + root. (Remember that when we reduplicate the first syllable of the root, we only use the first consonant of that syllable.) Here are a few examples.

nagpa-practice/ nagpapraktis	*practices* (used for activities such as yoga, martial arts, etc.)
nagyo-yoga (yoga)	*practices yoga*
nagsa-soccer (soccer)	*plays soccer*
nagte-tennis (tennis)	*plays tennis*

SENTENCE PRACTICE

Practice speaking/writing sentences about your daily schedule.

Ano ang ginagawa mo tuwing ...? *What do you do every(day) at*

_____?

6:00 a.m. – wake up
Gumigising ako nang alas-sais ng umaga.

6:15 a.m. – brush teeth
_____ **ako nang alas-sais kinse ng umaga.**

6:30 a.m. – take a bath/shower
_____ **ako nang** _____ **ng umaga.**

7:00 a.m. – eat breakfast
_____ **ako nang** _____
ng umaga.

7:30 a.m. – go to the office
_____ **ako sa opisina nang**
_____.

8:30 a.m. – 4:30 p.m. – work
_____ **ako mula** _____ **hanggang** _____.

12:00 – 1:00 p.m. – eat lunch
_____ **ako ng tanghalian mula**
_____.

5:00 – 6:00 p.m. – practice yoga
_____ **ako ng yoga mula**
_____.

6:15 p.m. – go home
_____ **ng bahay nang**
_____.

6:45 p.m. – cook dinner
_____ **ako ng hapunan nang** _____.

7:30 p.m. – eat dinner
_____ **ako ng** _____ **nang** _____.

8:30 p.m. – watch television

_____ nang _____.

10:00 p.m. – sleep

_____ ako _____.

GRAMMAR

Practice the verb conjugation for the actor focus by filling out the following chart below the new verbs.

Root	Inf/Imp	Completed	Incompleted	Contemplated
sepilyo	magsepilyo	nagsepilyo	nasesepilyo	magsesepilyo
bihis	magbihis	nagbihis		magbibihis
luto	magluto		nagluluto	magluluto
linis	maglinis	naglinis	naglilinis	
pasyal	mamasyal	namasyal	namamasyal	mamamasyal
bili	bumili	bumili		bibili
lakad	maglakad lumakad		naglalakad lumalakad	maglalakad lalakad
takbo	tumakbo	tumakbo		tatakbo
sayaw	sumayaw		sumasayaw	sasayaw
kanta		kumanta	kumakanta	
basa			nagbabasa	magbabasa
praktis	magpraktis			magpapraktis
uwi	umuwi		umuuwi	

PLAYING GOLF

Ralph, Richard, and two other golf buddies are on their way to the golf course in Tagaytay. They are talking about how often they do their favorite activities.

Here are some words, phrases, and sentences you should learn to prepare for this dialogue. Most of the words below are adverbs of frequency.

gaano kadalas	*how often*
Gaano kadalas kayong naglalaro ng golf?	How often + you (plural) + play + **ng** + golf? *How often do you play golf?*
palagi	*always*
Palagi ba kayong pumupunta sa Tagaytay?	Always + **ba** + you + **na** + go + to + Tagaytay? *Do you always go to Tagaytay?*
madalas	*often*
mas madalas	*more often*
na	*that* (used here as a relative pronoun)
Sige, mas madalas na akong sasama sa inyo.	Okay, more often + that + I + **na** + go with + you. *Okay, I'll join you more often then.*
hindi naman	*not really*
minsan/paminsan-minsan	*sometimes*
bihira	*rarely*
Bihira akong maglaro ng tennis.	Rarely + I + **na** + play + **ng** + tennis. *I rarely play tennis.*
hindi kailanman	*never*
siguro	*perhaps*
isang beses	*once/one time*
dalawang beses	*twice/two times*
sa isang buwan	*in a month*
Siguro, isang beses sa isang buwan.	Perhaps + one + time + in + one + **na** + month. *Perhaps, once a month.*
Ganoon ba?	*Is that so?*

RALPH : **Gaano kadalas kayong naglalaro ng golf?** *How often do you play golf?*

RICHARD : **Madalas.** *Often.*

RALPH : **Palagi ba kayong pumupunta sa Tagaytay?** *Do you always go to Tagaytay?*

RICHARD : **Hindi naman, paminsan-minsan lang. Siguro, isang beses sa isang buwan.** *Not really, just sometimes. Perhaps, once a month.*

RALPH : **Ganoon ba? Sige, madalas na akong sasama sa inyo.** *Is that so? Okay, I will join you often.*

RICHARD : **Naglalaro ka ba ng tennis?** *Do you play tennis?*

RALPH : **Bihira akong maglaro ng tennis.** *I rarely play tennis.*

GRAMMAR AND CONVERSATION PRACTICE

In the dialogue above, we learned the question:

Gaano kadalas kayong naglalaro ng golf? *How often do you play golf?*

Here are similar questions about activities:

Gaano kadalas kang naglalaro ng tennis? *How ofen do you play tennis?*

Gaano kadalas kang pumupunta sa Farmers' Market? *How often do you go to the Farmers' Market?*

Gaano kadalas kang nag-eensayo ng piano? *How often do you practice the piano?*

Possible responses to the questions above are:

Palagi akong naglalaro ng tennis. *I always play tennis.*

Madalas akong nagpupunta sa Farmers' Market. *I often go to the Farmers' Market.*

Nag-eensayo ako ng piano paminsan-minsan. *I sometimes play the piano.*

> **GRAMMAR TIP** What is the difference between these two sentences?
> <u>Madalas</u> akong <u>nagpupunta</u> sa Farmers market.
> Often + I + **na** + go + to + Farmers' Market.
> <u>Madalas</u> akong <u>magpunta</u> sa Farmers' Market.
> Often + I + **na** + to go + to + Farmers' market.
> Both mean "I often go to the Farmers' market." However, note the use of the incompleted aspect in **madalas nagpupunta** (*often go*) and the use of the infinitive form in **madalas magpunta** (literally, *often to go*). Think of this simply as a choice—you can translate an English sentence in two ways in Tagalog.
> In English, with adverbs of frequency we use the present tense. For example, we can say, "I cook vegetables often" or "I seldom watch films." However, there there are no tenses in Tagalog, only aspects (completed, incompleted, contemplated). Thus, when we use adverbs of frequency, we can use the incompleted aspect of the verb because the action has not yet been completed, and also the infinitive form, because we pair adverbs of frequency with verbs in the same way we pair modal verbs with verbs. For example, **gustong magpunta** (*want to go*) is structurally similar to **madalas magpunta** (*often go*).

QUESTION AND ANSWER PRACTICE

Practice the verbs you have learned in the chapter, and adverbs of frequency by asking and answering the following questions.

1. Question: **Gaano kadalas kang nagluluto?**

   Answer: _____ **akong nagluluto.**

2. Question: **Gaano kadalas kang nag-eehersisyo?**

   Answer: _____ **akong** _____.

3. Question: **Gaano kadalas kang nanonood ng telebisyon?**

   Answer: _____.

4. Question: _____ **kang nagpapraktis ng yoga?**

   Answer: **Madalas akong nagpapraktis ako ng yoga.**

5. Question: _____?

   Answer: **Bihira akong mamasyal sa parke.**

SUMMING UP

Practice talking/writing about your daily activities. What time do you wake up? What do you do after waking up? What do you usually do on weekends? Practice talking/writing about activities you often, sometimes, and rarely do.

_____

_____

_____

_____

_____

_____

_____

_____

_____

_____

CHAPTER 13

What would you like to eat?
Ano ang gusto mong kainin?

In this chapter, you will learn how to order food and drink at a restaurant and how to use adjectives to talk about food. You will also practice using helping verbs and the incompleted aspect of the verb for speaking/writing about what you are doing at the present.

At Dinner

Ralph and Melissa are having dinner in a restaurant. They are looking at a menu and giving their orders to the waiter.

kainin	*to eat*
gusto mong kainin	*you want/would like to eat*
Ano ang gusto mong kainin?	What + **ang** + want + you + **na** + to eat? *What would you like to eat?*
inumin	*to drink*
gusto niyong inumin	*you want/would like to drink*
Ano ang gusto niyong inumin?	What + **ang** + want + you + **na** to drink? *What would you like to drink?*
gutom	*hungry*
gutom na gutom	*very hungry*
Naku, gutom na gutom na ako.	Oh + very hungry + already + I. *Oh, I'm very hungry.*
gusto kong kumain	*want/would like to eat*
kanin	*rice*
sinigang na salmon	*salmon in sour broth*
adobong manok	*chicken stewed in vinegar*
leche flan	*milk custard*
Gusto kong kumain na salmon, adobong manok at leche flan.	Want + I + **na** + to eat + rice + salmon in sour broth + chicken **adobo** + and + milk custard. *I would like to eat rice, salmon in sour broth, chicken **adobo**, and milk custard.*

busog	*full*
pa	*still* (also means *yet*)
busog pa ako	*I am still full*
pero	*but*
rin	*also*
Busog pa ako pero gusto ko rin ng sinigang na. salmon	Full + still + I + but + like + I + also + **ng** + salmon in sour broth. *I am still full but I would also like some salmon in sour broth.*
pakibigyan	*please give (us)*
tubig	*water*
lang	*just*
Tubig lang ako.	Water + just + me. *Just water for me.*

RALPH : **Ano ang gusto mong kainin, Melissa?**
What would you like to eat, Melissa?

MELISSA : **Naku, gutom na gutom na ako. Gusto kong kumain ng kanin, sinigang na salmon, adobong manok at leche flan. Ikaw?** *Oh, I am very hungry. I would like rice, salmon in sour broth, chicken* **adobo** *and milk custard. What about you?*

RALPH : **Busog pa ako pero gusto ko rin ng sinigang na salmon.**
I am still full but I would also like some salmon in sour broth.

WAITER : **Ano ho ang order niyo?** *What is your order?*

RALPH : **Pakibigyan mo kami ng kanin, sinigang na salmon, adobong manok at leche flan.** *Please give us rice, salmon in sour broth, chicken* **adobo** *and milk custard.*

WAITER : **Ano ho ang gusto niyong inumin?**
What would you like to drink?

MELISSA : **Tubig lang ako.** *Just water for me.*

RALPH : **Iced tea na lang.** *Just iced tea.*

VOCABULARY

Here are the names of some common Filipino dishes and drinks, as well as words you can use for ordering in a restaurant.

sinangag	*fried rice*

sinigang na baboy	*pork in sour broth*
kare-kare	*meat and vegetables in peanut sauce*
prito	*fried*
isda	*fish*
pritong isda	*fried fish*
nilaga	*boiled*
baka	*beef*
nilagang baka	*boiled beef*
inihaw	*grilled/roasted*
manok	*chicken*
inihaw na manok	*grilled/roasted chicken*
guisado	*sauteed*
pansit	*noodle*
bihon	*rice noodles*
guisadong pansit bihon	*sauteed rice noodles*
pinasingaw	*steamed*
gulay	*vegetables*
pinasingaw na gulay	*steamed vegetables*
ensalada	*salad*
kamatis	*tomatoes*
sibuyas	*onions*
ensaladang kamatis at sibuyas	*tomato and onion salad*
sopas	*soup*
sabaw	*broth*
panghimagas	*dessert*

CULTURE TIP (Filipino food) Filipino food such as **sinigang** (sour soup) and **kare-kare** are very similar to foods found in Southeast Asia. Filipino food has also been influenced through trade with China as we can see in noodle dishes (**pansit**), and through colonization, as we can see in dishes such as **adobo** and *paella* from Spain and American fast food chains. However, Filipinos adapt foreign dishes to their taste. For example, in the Philippines the Italian spaghetti, introduced by Americans, has a sweet sauce made from tomato sauce and ketchup, and features ground meat and hotdogs.

GRAMMAR

Expressing Likes and Dislikes

We use the words **gusto** (*want; like; would like*) and **ayaw** (*dislike; doesn't want*) to express likes and dislikes. In the dialogue earlier, you learned that these words can be used both with nouns and with verbs.

First, let us look at using **gusto** with a noun, in this case, **sinigang na salmon**.

Gusto ko rin ng sinigang na salmon.   *I would also like some salmon in sour broth.*

 Note the use of marker **ng**—which marks salmon as the object (that which the speaker likes). Similarly, when we order in a restaurant, we can say the following sentences.

Gusto ko ng pizza.   *I would like some pizza.*
Gusto ko ng sandwich.   *I would like a sandwich.*

What happens when we replace **ng** with the marker **ang**? The meaning of the sentence changes, and the object also becomes the focus of the sentence. The speaker is now commenting on the food.

Gusto ko ang pizza.   *I like the pizza.*
Gusto ko ang sandwich.   *I like the sandwich.*

We can also use **gusto** with a verb in the infinitive form. In the sentence below, the verb is **kumain** (root word **kain**; to eat).

Gusto kong kumain ng kanin, sinigang na salmon at adobong manok at leche flan.   *I would like rice, salmon in sour broth, chicken* **adobo** *and milk custard.*

Similarly, we can say:

Gusto kong uminom ng tubig.   *I would like to drink water.*
Gusto kong mag-order.   *I would like to order.*

We can use **ayaw** (*dislike; don't want*) in the same manner. Study the following sentences.

Ayaw ko ng pizza.   *I don't want pizza.* (meaning either the person doesn't like pizza or doesn't want to order pizza).
Ayaw ko ang pizza. *I don't like the pizza.* (referring to the pizza the person is eating or pizza as a kind of food).

Ayaw kong kumain ng pizza.   *I don't want to eat pizza.*

Remember the following:

1. Use **ng** before the noun if you want to say "would like" or "don't want":

   Gusto ko ng sandwich.   *I would like a sandwich.*

   Ayaw ko ng sandwich.   *I don't want to have a sandwich.*

2. Use **ang** before the noun if you want to say that you like or don't like the particular food you are eating.

   Gusto ko ang sandwich.   *I like the sandwich.*

   Ayaw ko ang sandwich.   *I don't like the sandwich.*

3. Use **gusto** and **ayaw** with the infinitive form of the verb.

   Gusto kong kumain ng sandwich.   *I want to eat a sandwich.*

   Ayaw kong kumain ng sandwich.   *I don't want to eat a sandwich.*

DIALOGUE PRACTICE

Here is a menu from the fictitious restaurant **Kusina ni Nanay** (*Mother's Kitchen*). All the names of the dishes are in Tagalog. Some of the dishes have translations, and some do not, so you may need to refer to the vocabulary list above. In some cases, only translations for specific words are given (for example, **mangga** (*mango*)), but these words are paired up with words you have just learned (in this case, **ensalada**). You should be able to guess that **ensaladang mangga** is mango salad.

✳✳✳ KUSINA NI NANAY ✳✳✳

Gulay at Ensalada *Vegetables and Salads*

✳ Ensaladang mangga *(mango)*
✳ Ensaladang Talong *(eggplant)*
✳ Kangkong *(water spinach)* guisado
✳ Guinataang sitaw at kalabasa
   (stringbeans and squash cooked in coconut milk)
✳ Lumpiang sariwa *(fresh spring rolls)*

Mga Espesyal na Putahe *Special Dishes*
* Nilagang baka *(boiled beef)*
* Kare-kare
* Pritong tilapia
* Pinasingaw na lapu-lapu *(grouper)*
* Adobong manok at baboy
* Crispy pata *(leg of mutton)*
* Sinigang na hipon *(shrimp)*
* Inihaw na manok
* Lumpiang shanghai *(spring rolls with ground meat)*

Kanin at Pansit *Rice and Noodles*
* Kanin
* Sinangag *(fried rice)*
* Pancit bihon
* Pancit canton *(flour noodles)*
* Sotanghon *(bean thread noodles)* guisado

Mga Panghimagas at Inumin *Desserts and Drinks*
* Leche flan
* Halo-halo *(sweetened fruit in milk and ice)*
* Turon *(fried banana spring rolls)*
* Calamansi juice *(native lemon juice)*
* Mango juice
* Buko juice *(coconut water)*
* Kape
* Tsaa

Practice ordering food in a restaurant for the situations below.

Situation 1 You are in the restaurant alone. The waiter asks for your order. You are very hungry so you order a lot — water spinach, grilled chicken, **halo-halo** and mango juice.

WAITER : **Ano ho ang** _____?

YOU   : _____ **mo ako ng** _____.

WAITER : **Ano ho ang gusto niyong inumin?**

YOU   : _____ **na lang.**

WAITER : _____ ho ang gusto niyong panghimagas?

YOU : _____ na lang.

Situation 2 You are in the restaurant with your friend. Before eating, you ask your friend if she is hungry but she is still full. You would like to order fish and vegetables. She only wants to order sweetened fruit. You don't want dessert. You want to order juice while she would like some hot tea.

YOU : **Gutom ka ba?**

YOUR FRIEND : **Hindi.** _____**ako.**

WAITER : _____?

YOU : **Pakibigyan** _____.

WAITER : **Ano ho** _____ **panghimagas?**

YOUR FRIEND : _____.

YOU : **Ayaw ko ho ng** _____.

WAITER : _____**inumin?**

YOUR FRIEND : _____.

YOU : _____.

Situation 3 You are in the restaurant with your husband or wife. You like meat dishes while he/she is a vegetarian. You both have a sweet tooth so you order two desserts to share. You also order fried rice and two kinds of juice. You like the dessert you are eating.

_____

_____

_____

_____

_____

_____

_____

_____

GRAMMAR AND PRACTICE

Let us review the affix **paki-** (*please)* and study directional focus, this time using the affix **paki-** and -**an**.

Saying "please"

You have learned the use of **paki-** (*please*) in Chapter 9. In that chapter, words were formed by simply attaching **paki-** to the root word.

Review what you have learned by attaching **paki-** to the following words:

gawa (*make*) – _____

dala (*bring*) – _____

bili (*buy*) – _____

bukas (*open*) – _____

sara (*close*) – _____

kuha (*get*) – _____

Directional Focus with the affixes "paki-" and "-an"

Now, let us study the words **pakibigyan** and **pakibigay**. Both of these words have the same root, which is **bigay** (*give*). How do they differ?

Study the following sentences:

Pakibigyan mo ako ng adobo.   *Please give me some* **adobo.**
Pakibigay mo ang adobo sa akin.   *Please give the* **adobo** *to me.*

In the first sentence, the focus is on **ako** — the person to whom the action is directed to. We call this directional focus. In the second sentence, the focus is on **adobo**, the object. We know this because of the marker **ang**.

In previous chapters, you learned how to form verbs with directional focus using the affixes **in-** and -**an**. Let us now practice using **paki-** and -**an**, and study variations in conjugation.

With a root word that ends with a vowel, such as **dala** (*bring*), insert the letter "h" in between the word and the affix -**an**. Thus, the correct form of the word is **pakidalhan**, instead of **pakidalaan**. An exception to this rule is **kuha** (*get*). In this case, we use the letter "n" instead of "h," and say **pakikunan**.

Now, let use the same verbs from above to form **paki-** verbs with a directional focus. The first and last are done for you:

gawa – **pakigawan**

bili – _____

bukas – _____

sara – _____

dala – **pakidalhan**

Talking About Food

In this dialogue, Ralph and Melissa are almost done with their meal. They are talking about the food they are eating. Because they are in a hurry to catch a movie, they ask the waiter to give them the check before they finish dessert.

Here are some words and phrases used in this dialogue:

tamis	_sweet_ (root word)
Ang tamis!	_So sweet!_
Ang tamis ng leche flan!	**Ang** + sweet + **ng** + milk custard! _The milk custard is so sweet!_
masarap	_delicious_
napakaasim	_very sour_
magbayad	_pay_
Magbayad na tayo.	Pay + already + us. _Let's pay._
makuha	_get_
puwedeng makuha	_can get_
Excuse me po, puwede na ba naming makuha ang check?	Excuse me + **po**, can + already + **ba** + we + **na** + get + **ang** + check? _Excuse me, can we get the check?_
pakipirmahan	_please sign_
Pakipirmahan niyo lang po ito.	Please sign + you + just + **po** + this. _Just sign this please._

 **DIALOGUE B**

MELISSA : **Ang tamis ng leche flan!** *The milk custard is so sweet!*
RALPH : **Kumusta ang sinigang mo?** *How was your sinigang?*
MELISSA : **Masarap. Napakaasim.** *Delicious. Very sour.*
RALPH : **Magbayad na tayo.** *Let's pay.*
(Ralph calls the waiter.)
RALPH : **Excuse me po, puwede na ba naming makuha ang check?** *Excuse me, can we get the check?*
WAITER : **Heto po ang check niyo.** *Here is your check.*
RALPH : **Heto po ang credit card ko.** *Here is my credit card.*
WAITER : **Pakipirmahan niyo na lang po ito.** *Please sign this.*

> **CULTURE TIP (Using English Words)** As you now know, many English words are used in the Philippines. For example, it is more natural to say "Excuse me," rather than the more formal, **Mawalang-galang na ho** (literally, *Without any respect*). Also, we just use the words "check" and "credit card," since these concepts were non-existent in pre-colonial Philippines.

VOCABULARY

Here are ways to ask someone how the food was.

Kumusta ang leche flan mo? *How is your leche flan?*
Ano ang lasa ng leche flan mo? *What is the taste of your leche flan?*
Ano ang tingin mo sa leche flan nila? *What do you think of their leche flan?*
Masarap ba ang leche flan nila? *Is their leche flan delicious?*

Here are other adjectives, phrases, and sentences that describe food.

maanghang	*spicy*
maalat	*salty*
matabang	*bland*
malamig	*cold*
mainit	*hot*
mapait	*bitter*
mapakla	*tangy*
malasa	*tasty*

napakapait/mapait na mapait	*very bitter*
masyadong mapait	*too bitter*
Masarap ang lasa.	*The taste is delicious.*
Napakasarap ng sinigang.	*The **sinigang** is very delicious.*

To complain about food, one can say,

Malamig na ang sopas.	*The soup is cold.*
Masyadong mainit ang sopas.	*The soup is too hot.*
Hindi ko makain ang ampalaya.	*I cannot eat the bitter melon.*
Napakapait nitong ampalaya.	*This bitter melon is too bitter.*

GRAMMAR AND CONVERSATION PRACTICE

Intensifying adjectives

To intensify adjectives, or to say, for example, that bitter melon is "too bitter," or the custard is "too sweet," we can attach the affix **napaka-** to the root word. Usually, we use a hyphen when the root word starts with a vowel. Study the two examples and then write down the intensified adjectives for the others:

asim – napaka-asim

tamis – napakatamis

maalat – _____

lamig – _____

init – _____

To intensify the adjective, we can also double the adjective, putting **na** in between the two words. Remember to contract the linker **na** into **ng**, and then attach it to the end of the first word when the adjective ends with a vowel. This is shown in the second example below. Study the examples, and then write down the intensified adjectives for the remaining words.

masarap – masarap na masarap

malasa – malasang-malasa

maanghang – _____

mapait – _____

mapakla – _____

Finally, to intensify an adjective, we can put the word **masyadong** (contracted from **masyado na** meaning *very*) before it. Study the examples, and then write down the intensified adjectives for the remaining words.

mainit – **masyadong mainit**

maalat – **masyadong maalat**

matamis – _____

maanghang – _____

mapait – _____

Now, practice what you have just learned by asking and answering questions while pretending that you are in a restaurant. For this exercise, let us use food from other cuisines that you might be familiar with, so that you can easily think about the flavor of these foods.

1. Question: **Kumusta ang chicken wings mo?**

   Answer: _____?

2. Question: **Ano ang lasa ng cake mo?**

   Answer: _____?

3. Question: **Masarap ba ang pizza mo?**

   Answer: _____?

4. Question: _____?

   Answer: **Masyadong maalat.**

5. Question: _____?

   Answer: **Napaka-init ng sabaw ko.**

SUMMING UP

To practice what you have learned in this chapter, try to remember the last time you went to a restaurant. Talk or write about what you ordered and what the food tasted like.

_____

_____

_____

_____

_____

_____

_____

_____

_____

CHAPTER 14

Can you take me to the doctor?
Puwede mo ba akong samahan sa doktor?

In this chapter, we will learn about the parts of the body; we will talk about one's physical condition and feelings; and we will tell what one should and shouldn't do. We will also practice the imperative form of the verb.

Helping a Sick Friend

Meliisa is sick and she is in bed. Sarah is asking how she feels. She advises Melissa to see a doctor.

To prepare for this dialogue, study the following words and phrases.

masama	*bad; not well*
pakiramdam	*feeling*
Masama ang pakiramdam ko.	Bad + **ang** + feeling + I. *I am not feeling well.*
nararamdaman nararamdaman mo?	*what one feels* (used as a noun)
Ano ang	What + **ang** + feel + you? *How do you feel?*
masakit	*painful; hurting*
ulo	*head*
masakit ang ulo	*(my) head hurts*
barado	*stuffy*
ilong	*nose*
barado ang ilong	*(my) nose (is) stuffy*
Masakit ang ulo ko at barado ang ilong ko.	Hurts + **ang** + head + my + and stuffy + **ang** + nose + my. *My head hurts and my nose is stuffy.*
lagnat	*fever*
Naku, may lagnat ka!	Oh + have + fever + you! *Oh, you have a fever!*

samahan	*accompany*
Puwede mo ba akong samahan sa doktor?	Can + you + **ba** + me + **na** + accompany + to + doctor? *Can you take me to the doctor?*
tingin	*look* (root word)
magpatingin	*have someone take a look*
Magpatingin ka sa doktor.	Have (someone) take a look + you + by + doctor *We'll have the doctor take a look at you.*

 DIALOGUE A

SARAH : **Kumusta ka, Melissa?** *How are you, Melissa?*

MELISSA : **Masama ang pakiramdam ko.** *I am not feeling well.*

SARAH : **Ano ang nararamdaman mo?** *How do you feel?*

MELISSA : **Masakit ang ulo ko at barado ang ilong ko.** *My head hurts and my nose is stuffy.*

(*Sarah takes Melissa's temperature.*)

SARAH : **Naku, may lagnat ka!** *Oh, you have a fever!*

MELISSA : **Puwede mo ba akong samahan sa doktor?** *Can you take me to the doctor?*

SARAH : **Sige. Magpatingin ka na sa doktor.** *Okay. We'll have the doctor take a look at you.*

VOCABULARY

First, let us learn the names for some parts of the body.

buhok	*hair*
mata	*eye*
tenga	*ear*
bibig	*mouth*
ngipin	*teeth*
lalamunan	*throat*
balikat	*shoulder*
likod	*back*
dibdib	*chest/breast*
braso	*arm*
kamay	*hand*
daliri	*finger*
puso (accent on the first syllable)	*heart*

tiyan	*stomach*
baywang	*waist*
balakang	*hips*
hita	*thigh*
binti	*leg*
tuhod	*knee*
paa	*foot*
balat	*skin*

Now, let us study words that describe common illnesses.

sipon	*runny nose*
ubo	*cough*
trankaso	*flu*
nagsusuka	*vomiting*
nagtatae	*having diarrhea*
nasugatan	*is wounded/is hurt*
nahawa	*is infected*
nabali	*is broken* (for example, an arm or a leg)
napaso/nasunog	*got burned*

CONVERSATION PRACTICE

Here are some questions you can use to ask someone how he/she feels.

Kumusta ka?	*How are you?*
Ano ang nararamdaman mo?	*How do you feel?* (literally, *What are you feeling?*)
Ano ang pakiramdam mo?	*How do you feel?*

Note that in these sentences, we use the word **ano** (*what*), not **paano** (*how*).

Review the new words from the dialogue and the vocabulary words you have just studied and see how they are used in the following sentences that describe illnesses.

Masakit ang ulo ko.	*My head hurts.*
Masakit ang tiyan ko.	*My stomach hurts.*
May sipon ako.	*I have a runny nose.*
May trangkaso ako.	*I have the flu.*

Nagsusuka ako.	*I have been vomiting.*
Nasugatan ako sa braso.	*My arm is wounded.*
Nabalian ako ng paa.	*My leg is broken.*
Napaso ang kamay ko.	*My hand got burned.*

Laurie, Joy, Lean, Althea, Kaegy, and Tristan are all in the community health clinic. Laurie has the flu, Joy has a stomachache, Lean's ears are hurting, Althea burned herself while cooking, Kaegy keeps coughing, and Tristan fell down the stairs.

What are their responses to the doctor's question?

DOKTOR : **Ano ang nararamdaman mo?**

LAURIE : _____ .

JOY : _____ .

LEAN : _____ .

ALTHEA : _____ .

KAEGY : _____ .

TRISTAN : _____ .

GRAMMAR AND PRACTICE

Expressing action done by one person for another

In Chapter 10, you studied the affixes **magpa-** (actor focus), and **pina-** with **-an** (directional focus), for causative action or action caused by a person. This action can be a favor done, a request fulfilled, or a command.

Let us now study **ipa-** and **ipina-** affixes which are used when the focus is on the object. Then, let us compare the affixes all three focuses — actor (using **magpa-)**, object (using **ipa- or ipina-**), and directional (using **pina-** with **-in**).

When the focus is on the object, we can use the following formulas for **ipa-** and **ipina-** affixes:

root word — tingin *(examine; look)*

infinitive or imperative form – **ipa** + root word = **ipa** + **tingin** = **ipatingin**
completed aspect – **ipina-** + root word = **ipina** + **tingin** = **ipinatingin**
incompleted aspect – **ipina-** + first syllable of root word + root word =
  ipina + **ti** + **tingin** = **ipinatitingin**

contemplated – **ipa-** + first syllable of root word + root word = **ipa** + **ti** + **tingin** = ipatitingin

Study the following examples.

Ipatingin mo ang paa mo.	*Have your foot examined.*
Ipinatingin ko na ang paa ko.	*I had my foot examined.*
Ipinatitingin ko ang paa ko sa Philippine General Hospital.	*I have my foot examined at Philippine General Hospital.*
Ipatitingin ko ang paa ko sa Philippine General Hospital.	*I will have my foot examined at Philippine General Hospital.*

Here are more examples to compare actor, object and directional focus. In the first group of sentences, the focus is on the actor; in the second group, the focus is on the object; and in the third group, in the direction of the action.

Magpatingin ka ng paa sa doktor.	*Have the doctor examine your foot.* (imperative)
Nagpaluto ako ng chicken soup sa nanay ko para sa kapatid ko.	*I asked my mother to cook chicken soup for me.* (completed)
Nagpapagupit ako ng buhok sa Marconi's Hair Salon.	*I have my hair cut at Marconi's Hair Salon.* (incompleted)
Magpapagawa ako ng cake sa bakeshop para sa lolo ko.	*I will ask the bakeshop to make a cake for my grandfather.* (contemplated)
Ipatingin mo sa doktor ang paa mo.	*Have your foot examined by the doctor.* (imperative)
Chicken soup ang ipinaluto ko sa nanay ko para sa kapatid ko.	*Chicken soup is what I asked my mother to cook for my sister* (completed)
Ipinagugupit ko ang buhok ko sa Marconi's Hair Salon.	*My hair is what I have cut at Marconi's Hair Salon.* (incompleted)
Cake ang ipagagawa ko sa bakeshop para sa lolo ko.	*A cake is what I will have the bakeshop make for my grandfather.* (contemplated).
Patingnan mo ang paa mo sa doktor.	*Have your foot examined by the doctor.* (imperative)

Pinalutuan ko ng chicken soup sa nanay ko ang kapatid ko.	*My sister is who I asked my mother to cook the soup for.* (completed)
Pinagugupitan ko ang buhok sa Marconi's Hair Salon.	*My hair is what I have cut at Marconi's Hair Salon.* (incompleted)
Pinagawan ko ng cake sa bakeshop ang lolo ko.	*My grandfather is who I asked the bakeshop to make the cake for.* (contemplated)

Note that in the examples above, we can use both **ipatingin** and **patingnan** for the focus **paa** (*foot*), and both **ipinagugupit** and **pinagugupitan** for the focus **buhok** (*hair*). **Paa** and **buhok** are treated as the objects of the **ipatingin** and **ipinagugupit** sentences, and as the direction of the action in the **patingnan** and **pinagugupitan** sentences. However, the overall meaning of these sentences is the same.

Here are some charts showing how these verb forms are made.

Causative Verbs, actor focus

Root	Imperative	Completed	Incompleted	Contemplated
tingin *examine*	magpatingin	nagpatingin	nagpapatingin	magpapatingin
luto *cook*	magpaluto	nagpaluto	nagpapaluto	magpapaluto
gupit *cut* (hair)	magpagupit	nagpagupit	nagpapagupit	magpapagupit
gawa *make*	magpagawa	nagpagawa	nagpapagawa	magpapagawa

Causative Verbs, object focus

Root	Imperative	Completed	Incompleted	Contemplated
tingin *examine*	ipatingin	ipinatingin	ipinatitingin	ipatitingin
luto *cook*	ipaluto	ipinaluto	ipinaluluto	ipaluluto
gupit *cut* (hair)	ipagupit	ipinagupit	ipinagugupit	ipagugupit
gawa *make*	ipagawa	ipinagawa	ipinagagawa	ipagagawa

Causative Verbs, directional focus

Root	Imperative	Completed	Incompleted	Contemplated
tingin *examine*	patingnan	pinatingnan	pinatitingnan	patitingnan
luto *cook*	palutuan	pinalutuan	pinalulutuan	palulutuan
gupit *cut* (hair)	pagupitan	pinagupitan	pinagugupitan	pagugupitan
gawa *make*	pagawan	pinagawan	pinagagawan	pagagawan

Now, practice the use of these verbs in the following situations.

Situation 1 Kriya broke his arm so he went to the University Health Center to have it examined. He asked his mother to cook **sinigang** for him.

1. Question: **Saan nagpatingin so Kriya?**

   Answer: _____ si _____ sa _____

   _____.

2. Question: **Ano ang pinatingnan ni Kriya?**

   Answer: _____ ni Kriya ang _____

   _____niya.

3. Question: **Ano ang ipinaluto ni Kriya sa nanay niya?**

   Answer: _____ ang _____ ni Kriya
   sa nanay niya.

Situation 2 It is Paulene's birthday so she is going to Manila Hair Salon to have a haircut. Her sister Abby asked Manila Bakeshop to make a special chocolate cake for her.

4. Question: **Ano ang gagawin ni Paulene sa Manila Hair Salon?**

   Answer: _____ si Paulene sa _____

   _____.

5. Question: **Bakit magpapagupit si Paulene?**

   Answer: _____ si Paulene dahil _____

   _____.

6. Question: **Ano ang ipinagawa ni Abby para kay Paulene?**

   Answer: _____ ang _____ ni Abby para
   kay Paulene.

GRAMMAR TIP In spoken Tagalog, many Filipinos usually insert the syllable **pa** to the root word after the affix **pina-** when the want to say "have someone do something." For example, **luto** (*cook*) becomes **pinapaluto** (*have someone cook something for you*). However, in written Tagalog the first syllable of the root word is duplicated and the syllable **i** is inserted before the word. So, in written Tagalog, instead of using **pinapaluto** to say "*have someone cook something for you,*" you should write **ipinaluluto**.

At the Doctor's Office

Melissa is now at the doctor's office. She has told Dr. Araullo her symptoms and the doctor is giving her a prescription and advice.

inumin	*take medicine* (literally, *drink*)
tabletas	*tablets*
inumin mo ang mga tabletas	*take these tablets*
tatlong beses isang araw	*three times a day*
Inumin mo ang mga tabletas na ito nang tatlong beses isang araw.	Take + you + **ang** + tablets + **na** + this + **nang** + three + times + one + **na** + day. *Take these tablets three times a day.*
pumasok sa klase	*go to class* (literally, *enter class*)
bukas	*tomorrow*
Puwede na ho ba akong pumasok sa klase ko bukas?	Can + already + **ho** + **ba** + I + **na** + enter + to + class + my + tomorrow? *Can I go to class tomorrow?*
huwag	*don't*
muna	*yet*
Huwag ka munang pumasok sa klase.	Don't + you + yet + enter + to + class. *Don't go to class yet.*

dapat	*should*
magpahinga	*rest*
Dapat kang magpahinga.	Should + you + **na** + rest. *You should rest.*
dapat kong gawin	*have to do*
Ano pa ho ang dapat kong gawin?	What + else + **ho** + **ang** + should + I + **na** + do? *What else should I do?*
kailangan	*need*
kailangan mong pumunta	*need to go*
laboratoryo	*laboratory*
Kailangan mong pumunta sa laboratoryo.	Need + you + **na** + go + to laboratory. *You need to go to the laboratory.*
magpa-x-ray	*have an x-ray taken*
Magpa-xray ka roon.	Have x-ray taken + you + there. *Have your x-rays taken.*

 **DIALOGUE B**

Dr. Araullo : **Inumin mo ang mga tabletas na ito nang tatlong beses isang araw.** *Take these tablets three times a day.*

Melissa : **Puwede na ho ba akong pumasok sa klase ko bukas?** *Can I go to my class tomorrow?*

Dr. Araullo : **Huwag ka munang pumasok sa klase. Dapat kang magpahinga.** *Don't go to school yet. You should rest.*

Melissa : **Ano pa ho ang dapat kong gawin?** *What should I do [next]?*

Dr. Araullo : **Kailangan mong pumunta sa laboratoryo. Magpa-xray ka roon.** *You need to go to the laboratory to have x-rays taken.*

VOCABULARY AND GRAMMAR

The words **dapat** (*should*), **need** (*kailangan*), and **huwag** (*don't*) are used as modals or helping verbs.

To form a verb phrase, we put the pronoun **ka** (*you*) between the modal and the verb. For example,

dapat	*should*
dapat kang uminom	should + you + **na** + take. *you should take*
bitamina	*vitamins*

Dapat kang uminom ng bitamina.	Should + you + **na** + take + **ng** + vitamins. *You should take vitamins.*

However, when using a common or proper noun, the verb should follow the modal.

bata	*child*
mga bata	*children*
Dapat uminom ng bitamina ang mga bata.	*Children should take vitamins.*
hindi dapat	*should not*
ospital	*hospital*

We can also use **hindi dapat** (*shouldn't*) and **huwag** (*don't*).

Hindi dapat lumabas ng ospital si Mrs. Lim.	Should not + go out + **ng** + hospital + si + Mrs. Lim. *Mrs. Lim shouldn't go out of the hospital*
Huwag kang lumabas ng bahay.	*Do not go out of the house.*

Here are other words, phrases, and sentences you can use in talking about what one should and should't do when one is sick or when one wants to stay healthy.

araw-araw	*daily*
Dapat kang mag-ehersisyo araw-araw.	*You should exercise daily.*
Dapat kang kumain ng gulay.	*You should eat vegetables.*
alak	*liquor; alcohol*
Huwag kang uminom ng alak.	*Don't drink alcohol.*
magpa-eksamen	*have something examined*
dugo	*blood*
Kailangan mong magpa- eksamen ng dugo.	*You need to have your blood examined.*
mga nasa wastong edad	*adults*
mga matatanda/mga may edad na	*seniors*
regular	*regularly*
Dapat regular na nagpapatingin sa doktor ang mga matatanda.	*Seniors should regularly see a doctor.*

> **VOCABULARY TIP (Taking Medicine)** It may seem strange, but the word used to refer to taking medicine is **uminom** (*drink*). Remember, avoid doing literal translations. Instead, always consider that the things may be said differently in another language.

QUESTION AND ANSWER PRACTICE

First, let us practice asking about frequency. You can use the phrase, **Gaano kadalas** (*How often*).

1. Question: **Gaano kadalas ako dapat uminom ng gamot?**

   Answer: **Uminom ka ng gamot nang** _____.

2. Question: **Gaano kadalas ako dapat mag-ehersisyo?**

   Answer: _____ **ka nang** _____.

3. Question: **Gaano kadalas ako dapat uminom ng bitamina?**

   Answer: _____ **ka ng bitamina** _____.

Now, let us practice **dapat** (*should*), and **huwag** (*don't*).

4. Question: **Ano ang dapat kong kainin?**

   Answer: _____ **ng gulay.**

5. Question: **Ano ang dapat kong** _____?

   Answer: _____ **ka ng** _____.

6. Question: **Puwede ba akong uminom ng alak?**

   Answer: _____.

Finally, let us practice having something done by another.

7. Question: **Saan ako magpapa-x-ray?**

   Answer: _____ **ka sa** _____.

8. Question: **Ano ang dapat kong ipa-eksamen?**

   Answer: **Magpa-eksamen ka ng** _____.

SUMMING UP

Review what you have just learned in this chapter by talking/writing about your last visit to the doctor. Talk or write about your medical symptoms, the advice given by your doctor, and the medical tests you had to have taken.

CHAPTER 15

What is the weather like on Saturday?

Ano ang lagay ng panahon sa Sabado?

In this chapter, we will learn about the seasons and weather, the days of the week, and setting up appointments. For grammar, we will study the contemplated aspect of the verb, or how to talk about things you plan to do in the future.

Finalizing Plans

Ralph and Mr. Tolentino are having lunch at the office canteen. They are trying to finalize plans for a beach outing.

Study the following words, phrases, and sentences to prepare for the dialogue.

plano	*plan*
matutuloy	*will continue, still on*
matutuloy ang plano	*plans still on*
Sabado	*Saturday*
Matutuloy ba ang plano natin sa Sabado?	Still on + **ba** + **ang** plan + our + on + Saturday? *Are our plans still on for this Saturday?*
siguro	*perhaps*
hindi siguro	*perhaps not*
uulan	*will rain*
ayon sa	*according to*
balita	*news*
bagyo	*tropical storm*
Ayon sa balita, darating ang bagyo nang Sabado ng umaga.	According + to + news, arrive + tropical storm + on + Saturday + of + morning. *According to the news, the tropical storm will arrive on Saturday morning.*

susunod	*next*
susunod na Sabado	*next Saturday*
pumunta sa beach	*go to the beach*
Sa susunod na Sabado na lang tayo pumunta sa beach.	On + next Saturday + just + we + go + to + beach. *Let us just go to the beach next Saturday.*
Hindi ako puwede.	*I can't make it./I am not available.*
Hindi ako puwede sa susunod na Sabado.	*I can't make it next Saturday.*
bakit	*why*
dadalo	*attend*
kasal	*wedding*
Dadalo ako sa kasal ng kaibigan ko.	Attend + I + wedding + **ng** + friend + I. *I will attend my friend's wedding.*

DIALOGUE A

RALPH : **Matutuloy ba ang plano natin sa Sabado?** *Are our plans still on for this Saturday?*

MR. TOLENTINO : **Hindi siguro. Uulan sa Sabado.** *Perhaps not. It will rain on Saturday.*

RALPH : **Ayon sa balita, darating ang bagyo nang Sabado ng umaga.** *According to the news, the tropical storm will arrive on Saturday morning.*

MR. TOLENTINO : **Sa susunod na Sabado na lang tayo pumunta sa beach.** *Let us just go to the beach next Saturday.*

RALPH : **Hindi ako puwede sa susunod na Sabado.** *I cannot make it next Saturday.*

MR. TOLENTINO : **Bakit?** *Why?*

RALPH : **Dadalo ako sa kasal ng kaibigan ko.** *I will go to my friend's wedding.*

VOCABULARY

First, let us learn the names for the days of the week.

Lunes	*Monday*
Martes	*Tuesday*
Miyerkoles	*Wednesday*

Huwebes	*Thursday*
Biyernes	*Friday*
Sabado	*Saturday*
Linggo	*Sunday*

Now, let us learn other words we can use to describe the weather and seasons. Keep in mind that because the Philippines is a tropical country, there are really only two seasons: dry and wet.

panahon	*weather* (also *time*)
lagay ng panahon	*weather condition*
araw	*sun* (also *day*)
maaraw	*sunny*
ulan	*rain*
maulan	*rainy*
maulap	*cloudy*
maaliwalas	*not cloudy, not too hot*
mabanas	*humid*
maalinsangan	*hot and humid*
mahulimigmig	*hot, even when it's rainy*
maginaw	*cold*
mainit	*hot*
hangin	*wind*
malakas ang hangin	*winds are strong*
bumabagyo	*stormy*
tag-araw	*summer* (also *dry season*)
tag-ulan	*rainy* (also *wet season*)
tagsibol	*spring*
taglagas	*fall*
taglamig	*winter*

Finally, let us study some words you can use when talking about lifetime events and plans.

binyag	*baptism*
pagtatapos	*graduation*
anibersaryo	*anniversary*
libing	*funeral*
kanselado	*cancelled*
kanselado ang mga plano	*plans are cancelled*

QUESTION AND ANSWER PRACTICE

Practice asking and answering questions by talking about the dialogue.

1. Question: **Ano ang panahon sa Sabado?**

   Answer: _____ sa _____.

2. Question: **Ano ang sabi ng balita?**

   Answer: **Ayon sa** _____, _____ **ang**

   _____ **sa** _____.

3. Question: **Ano ang gagawin ni Ralph sa susunod na Sabado?**

   Answer: _____ **si** _____ **sa** _____

   sa susunod na _____.

Pretend that on Sunday it will be sunny, and that you will attend the baptism of your friend's daughter. However, according to the news, a storm will arrive in the evening and it will be windy and rainy. Answer the following questions.

1. Question: **Ano ang panahon sa Sabado?**

   Answer: _____.

2. Question: **Ano ang gagawin mo sa Linggo?**

   Answer: _____.

3. Question: **Ano ang lagay ng panahon sa gabi?**

   Answer: _____.

GRAMMAR AND CONVERSATION PRACTICE

The focus in this chapter is the contemplated aspect, or action that has yet to occur. The affixes used for the contemplated aspect depend on the focus of the sentence. Although you have been practicing the use of affixes for all aspects (imperative, completed, incomplete, contemplated) and three focuses (actor, object, directional), there are additional rules for some special verbs when they are used in the contemplated aspect.

As you have learned by now, the actor focus answers *who*-questions.

For verbs using **-um-** affixes, the contemplated aspect is formed by duplicating the first syllable of the root word. For example, the contemplated form of **gawa** (*make, do*) is **ga** + **gawa** = **gagawa.**

Sino ang gagawa ng cake para sa anibersaryo?	*Who will make a cake for the anniversary?*
Gagawa ako ng cake para sa anibersaryo.	*I will make a cake for the anniversary.*

For verbs using **mag-** affixes, the contemplated aspect is formed by chang-ing the "n" to "m" in the incompleted aspect. For example, **naglalaro** (play) = **maglalaro.**

Sino ang maglalaro ng tennis?	*Who will play tennis?*
Si Allen ang maglalaro ng tennis.	*Allen will play tennis.*

For verbs using **ma-/na-** affixes, the contemplated aspect is formed by **ma-** + first syllable of the root word + the root word. For example, **manonood** (watch) is formed by **ma** + **no** + **nood.**

Fill in the table below to practice conjugating verbs you have learned in previous chapters.

Actor Focus

Root Word	Inf/Imp	Completed	Incompleted	Contemplated
gawa *make, do*	gumawa			gagawa
laro *play, for games or sports*		naglaro	naglalaro	
punta *go*	pumunta		pumupunta	
pasok *go to school, work*	pumasok	pumasok		papasok
nood *watch*	manood		nanonood	

The object focus usually answers *what*-questions (and on rare occasions, *who*-questions).

The contemplated aspect is formed by duplicating the first syllable of the root word and attaching the affix **-in**. For example, as you have learned in Chapter 13, **kain** (*eat*) = **ka** + **kain** + **-in** = **kakainin.**

Ano ang gagawin mo para sa anibersaryo?	*What will you make for the anniversary?*
Cake ang gagawin ko para sa anibersaryo.	*It is a cake that I will make for the anniversary.*

Not all verbs have an object focus. For example, we usually ask only *who* and *where*, but not *what* for **punta** (*go*).

Sino ang pupunta?	*Who will go?*
Anong shopping mall ang pupuntahan mo?	*What shopping mall will you go to?*

Here are some other rules for the contemplated aspect of the object focus:

1. For root words ending in vowels, when the stress is either on the penultimate syllable or the last syllable and there is no glottal stop at the end of the word, add "h" to the end of the root before adding -**in**. For example, **bisita** = **bi** + **bisita** + **h** + -**in** = **bibisitahin**.

2. For root words ending in vowels and there is a glottal stop at the end of the word, add -**in**. For example, **laro** (play) = **la** + **laro** + **in** = **lalaruin**. However, note that in **laruin**, the "o" has been changed into "u." See the explanation for this in rule number 3.

3. For root words ending with "o" in the last syllable, convert the "o" to "u" before attaching -**in** to the root. A few examples are: **laro** (play) = **la** + **laro** + -**in** = **lalaruin**, and **inom** (*drink*) = **i** + **inom** + -**in** = **iinumin**.

4. For some words ending in a vowel, the contemplated form results in the removal of a phoneme (distinct unit of sound in a language). In the case of **bili**, for example, which ends with "i," remove the "i" and replace it with "h." For example, **bili** = **bi** + **bili** + -**in** = **bibilhin**. In the case of **gawa**, which ends with "a," simply remove one "a": **gawa** = **ga** + **gawa** + **in** = **gagawin**.

5. For root words ending with the "d," change the "d" into "r" if attaching an affix starting with a vowel. For example, **panood** = **pa** + **no** + **nood** + -**in** = **panonoorin**. The "d" in **nood** is changed into "r." We do not say **panonoodin** but **panonoorin**. The object focus for **nood** (**pinanood, pinanonood, panonoorin**) is also a special case because of the attachment of the affix **pa-**, thus forming **pina-**.

Object focus

Root	Inf/Imp	Completed	Incompleted	Contemplated
gawa *make,do*	gawin	ginawa	ginagawa	gagawin
laro *play,* for games or sports	laruin	nilaro	nilalaro	lalaruin
nood/panood *watch*	panoorin	pinanood	pinanonood	panonoorin
bisita *visit*	bisitahin	binisita	binibisita	bibisitahin

Directional focus refers to the location or direction of the action (for example, the event you will attend or the receiver of the action). The contemplated aspect is formed by duplicating the first syllable of the root word, adding it to the root word, and then adding the affix -an. Additional rules are similar to the rules for verbs in sentences where the focus is on the object of the sentence.

1. For root words ending in vowels, when the stress is either on the penultimate syllable or the last syllable, add "h" to the end of the root before adding -an. For example, **punta** (*go*) = pu + punta + h + -an = **pupuntahan.**

2. For root words ending in vowels and there is a glottal stop at the end of the word, just add -an. For example, gawa (make): **gawa** = ga + gawa + -an = **gagawan.**

3. Additionally, for some words ending in a vowel, such as **bili** (*buy*) and **gawa** (*make*) the contemplated form results in the removal of a phoneme (distinct unit of sound in a language). In the case of **bili**, for example, which ends with "i", remove the "i" and replace it with "h." For example, **bili** = bi + bili + -an = **bibilhan.**

4. When the root word ends in the vowel "o," for example, **dalo** (*attend*), "o" is converted into "u" and "h" is added: **dadaluhan** = da + dalo + -an = **dadaluhan.**

Ano ang gagawan mo ng cake?	*What will you make the cake for?*
Gagawan ko ng cake ang anibersaryo.	*I will make a care for the anniversary.*
Sino ang gagawan mo ng cake?	*Who will you make a cake for?*
Gagawan ko ng cake ang lola ko.	*I will make a cake for my grandmother.*

Some verbs, such as **laro** (*play*) and **nood/panood** (*watch*), do not have a directional focus.

Directional Focus

Root	Inf/Imp	Completed	Incompleted	Contemplated
gawa *make, do*	gawan	ginawan	ginagawan	gagawan
punta *go*	puntahan	pinuntahan	punupuntahan	pupuntahan
pasok *go to school, work*	pasukan	pinasukan	pinapasukan	papasukan
dalo (*attend*)	daluhan	dinadaluhan	dinadaluhan	dadaluhan

Below is your schedule for the next week. There are two columns: in the first, a fictitious schedule has been filled out for you. Fill out the second column yourself with your real schedule.

DAYS OF THE WEEK	WEEK 1	WEEK 2
LUNES	will go to work	
MARTES	wil watch a movie	
MIYERKULES	will play tennis	
HUWEBES	will go to the gym	
BIYERNES	will make a cake	
SABADO	will attend an anniversary party	
LINGGO	will visit grandmother	

Now, let us practice the verbs above by asking and answering questions:

1. Question: **Ano ang gagawin mo sa Huwebes?**

    Answer: _____ ako sa _____ sa _____.

2. Question: **Ano ang gagawin mo sa Lunes?**

    Answer: _____ ako sa _____ sa _____.

3. Question: **Ano ang dadaluhan mo sa Sabado?**

   Answer: _____ **ang dadaluhan ko sa Sabado.**

4. Question: **Sino ang bibisitahin mo sa Linggo?**

   Answer: _____ **ko ang** _____ **ko sa Linggo.**

5. Question: **Ano ang panonoorin mo sa Martes?**

   Answer: _____ **ko ang pelikulang** _____
   sa Martes.

6. Question: **Ano ang gagawin mo sa Biyernes?**

   Answer: **Gagawa ako ng** _____.

7. Question: **Ano ang gagawin mo sa susunod na Miyerkules?**

   Answer: _____.

8. Question: **Ano ang gagawin mo sa susunod na Lunes?**

   Answer: _____.

9. Question: **Ano ang gagawin mo sa susunod na Huwebes?**

   Answer: _____.

10. Question: **Ano ang gagawin mo sa susunod na Linggo?**

    Answer: _____.

GRAMMAR TIP (Switching Focus) The object and directional focuses can be more difficult to master than the actor focus. However, keep in mind that when you are asked a *what*-question using **ano**, your answer can use the actor focus. For example, in No. 6 of the exercise above, the verb in the question is **gagawin** but the verb in the answer is **gagawa**.

Setting up an Interview

Melissa wants to interview Mr. Tolentino for a class paper. She calls him to ask for an appointment. For this dialogue, review the use of formal language using honorifics such as **po and ho** (both of which are inserted in the sentence to show formality) and **opo** (yes) and **oho** (yes). Remember that there is no real difference between **po** and **ho**, and between **opo** and **oho**, although **po** and **opo** are considered to be more formal.

sana	*hope*
gusto ko sana	*I hope to/ I would like to*
mag-set	*to set up*
interbyu	*interview*
mag-set ng interbyu	*set up an interview*
Gusto ko ho sanang mag-set ng interbyu sa inyo.	Want + I + **ho** + hope + set up + **ng** + interview + with + you. *I hope to set up an interview with you.*
para saan	*for what*
Para saan ito?	For what + this? *For what?*
Para po sa klase ko.	*For my class.*
puwede	*available* (also, *can*)
Puwede po ako.	*I am available. / I can make it.*
Puwede po ba kayo sa Miyerkoles ng umaga?	Available + **po** + **ba** + you + on + Wednesday + of + morning? *Are you available on Wednesday morning?*
Naku, may meeting ako sa Miyerkules.	Oh no + have + meeting + I + on Wednesday. *Oh no, I have a meeting on Wednesday.*
libre	*free*
Libre ka ba sa Huwebes ng hapon?	Free + you + **ba** + on Wednesday + of afternoon? *Are you free on Wednesday afternoon?*
pupuntahan	*will come/will go*
Pupuntahan ko po ba kayo sa opisina ninyo?	Will come + I + **po** + **ba** + you + in office + your? *Should I come to your office?*
magkita	*meet/see*
Magkita tayo sa opisina ko.	Meet + us + in + office + my. *Let's meet in my office.*

MELISSA	:	**Magandang umaga po, Mr. Tolentino.**
		Good morning, Mr. Tolentino.
MR. TOLENTINO	:	**Magandang umaga rin.** *Good morning too.*
MELISSA	:	**Gusto ko po sanang mag-set ng interbyu sa inyo.**
		I *hope to set up an interview with you.*
MR. TOLENTINO	:	**Para saan ito?** *For what?*
MELISSA	:	**Para po sa klase ko. Puwede po ba kayo sa Miyerkoles ng umaga?** *For my class. Are you available on Wednesday morning?*
MR. TOLENTINO	:	**Naku, may meeting ako sa Miyerkoles. Libre ka ba sa Huwebes ng hapon?** *Oh, I have a meeting on Wednesday. Are you free on Wednesday afternoon?*
MELISSA	:	**Puwede po ako. Pupuntahan ko po ba kayo sa opisina niyo?** *I can make it. Should I come to your office?*
MR. TOLENTINO	:	**Oo. Magkita tayo sa opisina ko.** *Yes. Let's meet in my office.*

VOCABULARY AND GRAMMAR

Asking questions

There are several ways to ask the same question. For example, if you want to talk to or interview someone, you can say:

Puwede ba kitang maka-usap?	*Can I talk to you?*
Puwede ba kitang ma-interbyu?	*Can I interview you?*
Puwede ba tayong mag-set up ng interbyu?	*Can we set up an interview?*
Puwede ba tayong mag-iskedyul ng interbyu?	*Can we schedule an interview?*

Setting up a meeting/appointment

Note the use of words derived from English, such as **interbyu** (*interview*), **mag-set** (*set*) and **mag-iskedyul** (*schedule*).

Do not confuse the following words:

magkita	*to meet; to see each other*
pulong	*meeting* (as in a group meeting)
magpupulong	*hold a meeting*
magtagpo	*to meet up*
tagpuan	*meeting place*

Thus, you can say the following:

Saan tayo magkikita?	*Where will we see each other?*
Saan tayo magtatagpo?	*Where will we meet up?*
Saan ang tagpuan natin?	*Where is our meeting place?*
Saan tayo magpupulong?	*Where will we have our meeting?*
Saan ang miting ng grupo natin?	*Where is our group meeting?*

Cancelling/Postponing an appointment

Here are words, phrases and sentences you can use to say you cannot make it, to propose another meeting date, or to schedule a call to confirm the appointment.

abala	*busy*
Abala ako sa Lunes.	*I am busy on Monday.*
May gagawin ako sa _____.	*I am doing something on _____.*

lakad	used to mean *have somewhere to go to* (literally, *to walk*)
May lakad ako sa Martes.	*I have somewhere to go to on Tuesday.*
tatawagan	*will call*
uli/muli	*again*
kumpirmahin	*to confirm*
Tatawagan kitang muli para kumpirmahin ang pagkikita natin.	Call + I + **na** + again + to + confirm + **ang** + meeting + our. *I will call you again to confirm our appointment.*

Expressing conditionality

Use the words **kung** (*if*) and **kapag** (*when*) to express conditionality.

kung	*if*
Tawagan mo ako kung puwede ka.	*Call me if you can make it.*
Kung hindi ka puwede, tawagan mo ako.	*If you cannot make it, call me.*
Kapag nakuha mo ang message na ito ...	*When you get this message ...*
Magkita tayo kapag libre ka na.	*Let's meet when you are free.*

CONVERSATION PRACTICE

Here are two situations. Practice what you have just learned by asking and answering questions. The first situation is with a client, so you should use formal language. The second one is with a friend, so you should use informal language.

Situation 1 You want to schedule an interview with a client to determine her company's needs. You offer to meet her on Thursday but she is busy. She asks to meet with you on Friday afternoon, but you have somewhere to go to and can only make it in the morning. You are meeting at her office. She may be on another floor, so she asks you to call her when you get to the building.

You : Puwede _____?

Your client : Pasensiya ka na. _____.

Puwede ka ba sa _____?

YOU   : May _____ po ako sa _____.

YOUR CLIENT : **Kailan ka puwede?**

YOU   : _____.

             Saan po tayo _____?

YOUR CLIENT : _____ **tayo sa** _____.

YOU   : **Sige po.**

YOUR CLIENT : **Tawagan mo ako** _____ **dumating ka na sa building.**

Situation 2 You want to set up a meeting with members of your class to talk about a project. You first call one classmate to ask if he is available on Saturday afternoon. He is not available, so he suggests Sunday morning. You are doing something in the morning but you are available in the afternoon. You tell him that you will call up your other classmate to confirm her availability. He asks you to call him if the other classmate confirms.

YOU   : _____?

CLASSMATE : _____. **Hindi ako** _____

             pero _____.

YOU   : **May** _____ **ako sa** _____ **pero**

             _____.

CLASSMATE : **Puwede ako sa** _____.

YOU   : **Sige, tatawagan ko ang kaklase natin para** _____

             kung libre rin siya.

CLASSMATE : **Sige,** _____**kapag nagkumpirma na siya.**

YOU   : **Saan ang magandang tagpuan?**

CLASSMATE : _____ **tayo sa University Café.**

SUMMING UP

To practice what you have learned in this chapter, talk/write about your plans and activities for the coming week. You can also talk/write about your next meeting/appointment – when, where, and whom you are meeting.

_____

_____

_____

_____

_____

_____

_____

_____

_____

_____

CHAPTER 16

Can I rent this apartment?
Puwede ko bang upahan ang apartment na ito?

Available Apartments

Ralph Woods is looking at apartments in the city of Manila He is meeting with a rental agent.

Study the following words, phrases, and sentences to prepare for the dialogue.

upa	*rent* (noun)
upahan	*to rent* (verb)
puwede kong upahan	*can rent*
May apartment po ba kayo na puwede kong upahan?	Have + apartment + **po ba** + you + that + can + I + rent? *Do you have an apartment that I can rent?*
bakante	*vacant*
May dalawang bakanteng apartment ho kami.	*We have two vacant apartments.*
tingnan	*look, see*
Gusto ho ba ninyong tingnan?	Want + **ho** + **ba** + you + look? *Would you like to see it?*
ilan	*how many*
kuwarto	*rooms*
Ilan ho ang kuwarto?	How many + **ho** + **ang** + room? *How many rooms are there?*
May dalawang kuwarto ho sa apartment na ito.	*There are two rooms in this apartment.*
na	used to mean *as*

Puwede ho niyong gamitin na opisina ang isang kuwarto.	Can + **ho** + you + **na** + use + as + office + **ang** + one + room. *You can use one room as an office.*
na	used to mean *that* (relative pronoun)
gamit	*things, equipment*
kusina na kumpleto sa gamit	kitchen + that + complete + in equipment *fully furnished kitchen*
May sala, banyo, at kusina na kumpleto sa gamit.	*There is a living room, one bathroom, and a fully furnished kitchen.*
buwan	*month*
kada buwan	*per month*
Magkano ho ang upa kada buwan?	How much + **ho** + **ang** + rent + per + month? *How much is the rent per month?*
beinte mil	*twenty thousand*
kada buwan	*per month*
Beinte mil ho ang upa kada buwan.	Twenty thousand + **ho** + **ang** + rent + per + month. *The rent is twenty thousand a month.*
kukunin	*will get, will take*
Sige, kukunin ko ho ang apartment.	*Okay, I'll take the apartment.*
puwedeng lumipat	*can move, can move in*
Kailan ho ako puwedeng lumipat?	When + **ho** + I + can + **na** + move in? *When can I move in?*
handa	*ready*
susunod na buwan	*next month*
Handa na ho ito sa susunod na buwan.	Ready + already + **ho** + this + on next + **na** + month. *The apartment will be ready next month.*
Mayo	*May* (the month)
Puwede na kayong lumipat sa Mayo.	*You can move in May.*

DIALOGUE A

RALPH : **May apartment ho ba kayo na puwede kong upahan?**
Do you have an apartment I can rent?

RENTAL AGENT : **May dalawang bakanteng apartment ho kami. Gusto ho ba ninyong tingnan?** *We have vacant apartments. Would you like to see one?*

RALPH : **Oho. Ilan ho ang kuwarto?** *Yes. How many rooms are there?*

RENTAL AGENT : **May dalawang kuwarto ho sa apartment. Puwede ho ninyong gamitin na opisina ang isang kuwarto. May sala, isang banyo, at kusina na kumpleto na sa gamit.** *There are two bedrooms in the apartment. You can use one room as an office. There is a living room, one bathroom, and a fully furnished kitchen.*

RALPH : **Magkano ho ang upa kada buwan?** *How much is the rent per month?*

RENTAL AGENT : **Beinte mil ho ang upa sa isang buwan.** *The rent is 20,000 pesos a month.*

RALPH : **Sige, kukunin ko ang apartment. Kailan ho ako puwedeng lumipat?** *Okay, I'll take the apartment. When can I move in?*

RENTAL AGENT : **Handa na ho ito sa susunod na buwan. Puwede na ho kayong lumipat sa Mayo.** *This (apartment) will be ready next month. You can (already) move in May.*

RALPH : **Salamat po!** *Thank you!*

VOCABULARY

First, let us learn the names for the months of the year.

Buwan	Month
Enero	*January*
Pebrero	*February*
Marso	*March*
Abril	*April*
Mayo	*May*
Hunyo	*June*

Hulyo	*July*
Agosto	*August*
Setyembre	*September*
Oktubre	*October*
Nobyembre	*November*
Disyembre	*December*

Now practice the dialogue again, this time substituting the new words you have learned.

GRAMMAR

Let us review the use of modals (helping verbs) and the actor focus.

Modals or Helping Verbs

Verbs with modals such as **gusto** (*want*), **kailangan** (*need*), and **puwede** (*can*) use the infinitive form. Study the following examples.

Sino ang gustong umupa ng bahay?	*Who wants to rent a house?*
Gustong umupa ng bahay ni Mr. Tolentino.	*Mr. Tolentino wants to rent a house.*
Saan niya gustong tumingin?	*Where does he want to look?*
Gusto niyang tumingin sa Manila.	*He wants to look in Manila.*
Kailan niya kailangang kumuha ng bahay?	*When does he need to get a house?*
Kailangan niyang kumuha ng bahay sa susunod na buwan.	*He needs to get a house next month.*
Kallan siya puwedeng lumipat?	*When can he move in?*
Puwede siyang lumipat sa Agosto.	*He can move in August.*

Study the following table, and see how these verbs are used in sentences.

Actor Focus

Root	Inf/Imp	Completed	Incompleted	Comtemplated
upa *rent*	umupa	umupa	umuupa	uupa
tingin *look*	tumingin	tumitingin	tumitingin	titingin
kuha *get*	kumuha	kumuha	kumukuha	kukuha
lipat *move*	lumipat	lumipat	lumilipat	lilipat

Gusto kong umupa ng apartment.

I want to rent an apartment.

Tumingin ako ng apartment kahapon.

I looked at an apartment yesterday.

Kumukuha si Melissa ng apartment.

Melissa is getting an apartment.

Lilipat siya sa apartment sa Hunyo.

She will move to the apartment in June.

QUESTION AND ANSWER PRACTICE

Answer the following questions based on the dialogue you read.

1. Question: **Sino ang gustong umupa ng apartment?**

    Answer: _____

2. Question: **Saang lungsod siya tumitingin ng mga apartment?**

    Answer: _____

3. Question: **Kailan siya puwedeng lumipat?**

    Answer: _____

Don't Forget to Pay Rent!

Let us expand the dialogue between Ralph and the rental agent.

deposito	*deposit*
paunang bayad	*advance payment*
Magkano ang kailangang deposito at paunang bayad?	How much + **ang** + needed + deposit + and + advance payment? *How much deposit and advance payment are needed?*

Kailangan po ng isang buwang deposito at isang buwang paunang bayad.	Need + **ho** + **ng** + one + **na** + month + **na** + deposit + and + one + **na** + month **na** + advance payment. *We need one month's deposit and one month's advance payment.*
kasama	*included*
kuryente	*electricity*
Kasama na po ba ang kuryente, cable at internet sa upa?	Included + already + **po** + **ba** + **ang** electricity, + cable + and + internet + in + rent? *Are the electricity, cable and internet included in the rent?*
hiwalay	*separate*
Hiwalay po ang kuryente, cable at internet.	Separate + **po** + **ang** + electricity, cable + and + internet. *Electricity, cable, and internet are separate.*
Kasama na po ba ang gas at tubig sa upa?	*Are the gas and water and water included in the rent?*
Kasama na po sa upa ang gas at tubig.	*Gas and water are included in the rent.*

 **DIALOGUE B**

RALPH : **Magkano ang kailangang deposito at paunang bayad?**
How much deposit and advance payment are needed?

RENTAL AGENT : **Kailangan po ng isang buwang deposito at isang buwang paunang bayad.** *[We] need one month's deposit and one month's advance payment.*

RALPH : **Kasama na ho ba ang kuryente, cable, at internet sa upa?** *Are the electricity, cable, and internet included in the rent?*

RENTAL AGENT : **Hiwalay po ang kuryente, cable, at internet.**
The electricity, cable, and internet are separate.

RALPH : **Kasama na ho ba ang gas at tubig sa upa?**
Are the gas and water included in the rent?

RENTAL AGENT : **Kasama na po sa upa ang gas at tubig.**
The gas and water are included in the rent.

RALPH : **Mabuti naman.** *That's good.*

GRAMMAR

Study the following table of verbs using **in-** and **-an** affixes for directional focus.

Directional Focus

Root	Inf/Imp	Completed	Incompleted	Comtemplated
upa *rent*	upahan	inupahan	inuupahan	uupahan
tingin *look*	tingnan	tiningnan	tinitingnan	titingnan
kuha *get/take*	kunan	kinunan	kinukunan	kukunan
lipat *move*	lipatan	nilipatan	nililipatan	lilipatan

Study the sentences below and determine the directional focus of each verb.

Inupahan ni Ralph ang apartment noong Mayo.	*Ralph rented the apartment in May.*
Tinitingnan niya ang mga kuwarto.	*He is looking at the rooms.*
Kinukunan ng commission ang upa ni Ralph para sa rental agent.	*A commission is taken from Ralph's rent for the rental agent.*
Ito ang apartment na lilipatan ni Ralph.	*This is the apartment Ralph will move to.*

> **VOCABULARY NOTE (Changing Meanings)** Many Tagalog words have the same spelling, but different meanings. In the dialogue above, the word **kasama** is used as an adjective to describe the water and gas being *included* in the rent. The word **kasama** can also mean *companion* and *comrade*. And, if pronounced with the accent on the last syllable, it means a *peasant* or *farmer*.

QUESTION AND ANSWER PRACTICE

1. Question : **Ilang kuwarto ang apartment ni Ralph?**

   Answer: _____.

2. Question: **Magkano ang upa sa apartment ni Ralph?**

   Answer: _____.

3. Question: An ang puwedeng gawin ni Ralph sa isang kuwarto?

   Answer: _____.

4. Question: Magkano ang upa sa bawat buwan?

   Answer: _____.

5. Question: Ilang buwan bago puwedeng lumipat si Ralph?

   Answer: _____.

6. Question: Anong buwan puwedeng lumipat si Ralph?

   Answer: _____.

7. Question: Magkano ang kailangang deposit at pangunang bayad ni Ralph?

   Answer: _____

   _____.

8. Question: Ano ang kasama sa upa?

   Answer: _____.

9. Question: Ano ang mga hiwalay na bayad sa upa?

   Answer: _____.

10. Question: Saan pupunta si Ralph sa Mayo para sa susi?

    Answer: _____

    _____.

Nice Apartment!

Ralph is having a further conversation about the apartment with the rental agent.

aba	*so* (interjection)
malaki	*big*
pala	expression used to show surprise
Aba, malaki pala ang sala ng apartment na ito.	So + big + **pala** + **ang** + living room + **ng** + apartment + **na** + this. *Oh, the living room of this apartment is so big.*
imbita	*invite* (root word)
makakapag-imbita	*will be able to invite*

Makapag-iimbita ho kayo ng mga kaibigan ninyo.	Will be able to invite + **ho** + you + **ng** + friends + your. *You can invite your friends over.*
marami	*many*
maraming mga bintana	*many windows*
Maraming mga bintana sa sala.	Many + windows + in + living room. *There are a lot of windows in the living room.*
kaya	*and so, that is why*
maganda	*nice* (also means *beautiful)*
maliwanag	*bright*
Maraming mga bintana sa sala, kaya maganda at maliwanag.	Many + windows + in + living room + that is why + nice + and + bright. *There are a lot of windows in the living room, so it's nice and bright.*
bakit	*why*
madilim	*dark*
sa loob	*inside*
Bakit madilim sa loob ng banyo?	Why + dark + inside + of + bathroom? *Why is it dark inside the bathroom?*
kasi/dahil	*because*
pundido	*burnt out* (referring to light bulbs)
bumbilya	*light bulb*
Kasi ho, pundido ang bumbilya.	Because + **ho** + burnt out + **ang** + light bulb. *Because the light bulb burnt out.*
papalitan	*replace/change*
Papalitan ko ho.	Replace + I + **ho**. *I will replace it.*
malapit	*near*
sakayan ng bus	*bus stop*
Malapit ba ang bus stop sa apartment na ito?	Near + **ba** + **ang** + bus stop + to + apartment + **na** + this? *Is the bus stop near this apartment?*
naku	*oh* (interjection)
malayo	*far*

| Naku, malayo ho ang bus stop. | Oh, far + **ho** + **ang** + bus stop. *Oh, the bus stop is far.* |

DIALOGUE C

RALPH : **Aba, malaki pala ang sala ng apartment na ito.** *Oh, the living room of this apartment is big.*

RENTAL AGENT : **Oho. Makapag-iimbita ho kayo ng mga kaibigan ninyo.** *Yes. You can invite your friends over.*

RALPH : **Maraming mga bintana ang sala, kaya maganda at maliwanag.** *There are a lot of windows in the living room, so It's nice and bright.*

RENTAL AGENT : **Opo.** *Yes.*

RALPH : **Bakit madilim sa loob ng banyo?** *Why is it dark inside the bathroom?*

RENTAL AGENT : **Kasi ho, pundido ang bumbilya. Papalitan ko ho.** *That's because the light bulb burnt out. I'll replace it.*

RALPH : **Malapit ba ang bus stop sa apartment na ito?** *Is the bus stop near this apartment?*

RENTAL AGENT : **Naku, malayo ho ang bus stop.** *Oh, the bus stop is far.*

VOCABULARY

Adjectives

First, study the following adjectives that can be used to describe a place.

malaki	*big*
maliit	*small*
maliwanag	*bright*
madilim	*dark*
malapad	*wide*
makitid	*narrow*
malayo	*far*
malapit	*near*
mapanganib	*dangerous*
ligtas	*safe*

GRAMMAR

Expressing Cause and Effect

Next, study the following words and sentences that express cause and effect, in answer to questions using the word **bakit** (*why*). Note that there can be two or three ways of responding to a question.

kaya/kung kaya	*so, and so*
dahil/kasi	*because*

Question: **Bakit mo gusto ang apartment?** *Why do you like the apartment?*

Answer 1: **Gusto ko ang apartment dahil maliwanag.** *I like the apartment because it is bright.*

Answer 2: **Gusto ko ang apartment kasi maliwanag.** *I like the apartment because it is bright.*

In the answers above, **dahil** and **kasi** are used interchangeably. However, **kasi** is more colloquial while **dahil** is more formal.

Question: **Bakit maliwanag ang apartment?**
Why is the apartment bright?

Answer 1: **Maraming bintana kaya maliwanag ang apartment.**
There are many windows, so the apartment is bright.

Answer 2: **Maraming bintana kung kaya maliwanag ang apartment.**
There are many windows, and so the apartment is bright.

Answer 3: **Maliwanag ang apartment dahil maraming bintana.**
The apartment is bright because there are many windows.

Answer 4: **Dahil maraming bintana, maliwanag ang apartment.**
Because there are many windows, the apartment is bright.

There is no difference in the use of **kaya** and **kung kaya**. The word **kung** literally means *if*, but when paired with *kaya*, is used to mean *and*. In conversations, speakers tend to just use **kaya**.

Both **kaya/kung kaya** and **dahil/kasi** can be used in the middle of the sentence, between two clauses. For example,

Maraming bintana + kaya +	*There are many windows,*
maliwanag ang apartment.	*so the apartment is bright.*
Maliwanag ang apartment +	*The apartment is bright,*
dahil/kasi + maraming bintana.	*because there are many windows.*

However, only **dahil** can be used in the beginning of a sentence when there are two clauses. While **kasi** has exactly the same meaning (*because*), it is usually used only between clauses. However, **kasi** can be used at the beginning of a short response. For example,

Dahil + maraming bintana, maliwanag ang apartment.	*Because there are many windows, the apartment is bright.*
Kasi + maliwanag ang apartment.	*Because the apartment is bright.*

DIALOGUE PRACTICE

Use the adjectives and verbs you have learned, and practice the use of **kaya/kung kaya** (*so/and so*), **dahil** (*because*) and **kasi** (*because*). The root words of the verbs are provided in parenthesis. Create dialogues according to the following situations:

Situation 1 You are telling your friend about an apartment you recently leased. You chose this apartment because it is close to to a train station. It is also big, and bright.

YOUR FRIEND : _____ **(kuha) mo ba ang apartment?**

YOU   : _____.

YOUR FRIEND : **Bakit mo gusto ang apartment na ito?**

YOU   : **Gusto ko ang apartment** _____.

YOUR FRIEND : **Malapit ba ang apartment sa bus stop, o sa train station?**

YOU   : _____

_____

Situation 2 Mr. Tolentino is buying a new house. He is talking to a real estate agent and telling the agent that he wants a big house. He refuses the first house because it is near a river. He wants a house far from a river because it is safer from floods during storms. (Remember that the word for *don't like* is **ayaw**, as you have learned in Chapter 13.)

REAL ESTATE AGENT : **Ano hong bahay ang gusto niyo?**

MR. TOLENTINO   : _____.

REAL ESTATE AGENT : **Ito ho ang isang bahay.** (*Agent shows a picture.*)
Malaki ho ito at _____ **sa Marikina River.**

Mr. Tolentino : _____ ko sa bahay na ito.

Real Estate Agent : _____ ho?

Mr. Tolentino : _____ mas _____ kapag may bagyo.

> **CULTURE TIP (For Luck)** When someone moves to a new house, it is customary to bring rice, sugar, and salt when you first enter the house. During the blessing and house-warming party, uncooked rice and coins are showered in every room of the house. In the construction of houses, coins are buried with the foundation and sometimes also included with the flooring of the house. Coins are intentionally kept laying around on the floor in the corners of rooms. These customs are all thought to represent good luck, wealth, and abundance.

SUMMING UP

To review what you have learned in this chapter, talk/write about the house or apartment you would like to buy or rent.

_____

_____

_____

_____

_____

_____

_____

_____

_____

CHAPTER 17

Where are you going?
Saan ka pupunta?

In this chapter, study words for transportation and review actor, object and directional focus.

Melissa is waiting at the jeepney stop. Mr. Tolentino is passing by in his car.

I Need a Ride

Let us learn words, phrases, and sentences used when talk about transportation.

Saan ka pupunta?	*Where are you going?*
Pupunta po ako sa unibersidad.	Going + **po** + I + to + university. *I am going to the university.*
hintay	*wait* (root word)
hinihintay	*waiting* (object focus)
Ano ang hinihintay mo?	What + **ang** + waiting + you? *What are you waiting for?*
naghihintay	*waiting* (actor focus)
jeepney	*jeepney* (a custom-made Filipino vehicle made from a surplus US Army jeep)
Naghihintay po ako ng jeepney.	Waiting + **po** + I + **ng** + jeepney. *I am waiting for a jeepney.*
sabay	*concurrent* (rood word)
sumabay	used to mean *ride with*
na	used here for emphasis
Sumabay ka na sa akin.	Ride + you + **na** + with + me. *Just ride with me.*
malapit	*close/near*
dating (pronounced **da-ting**; stress on the second syllable)	*arrive* (root word)
nang	used to connect an adverb with a verb

malapit nang dumating	*will arrive soon* (literally, *close to arrive*)
Malapit nang dumating ang jeepney.	Close + **nang** + to arrive + **ang** + jeepney. *The jeepney will arrive soon.*
Sige na.	*Please.*
sakay	*ride, get on*
kotse	*car*
Sige na, sumakay ka na sa kotse.	Please + ride + you + already + in + car. *Please get in the car.*

DIALOGUE A

MR. TOLENTINO : **Melissa, ikaw pala! Kumusta ka?** *Melissa, it's you! How are you?*

MELISSA : **Mabuti naman po. Kumusta po kayo?** *I'm fine. How are you?*

MR. TOLENTINO : **Mabuti rin naman. Saan ka pupunta?** *I'm fine. Where are you going?*

MELISSA : **Pupunta po ako sa unibersidad.** *I am going to the university.*

MR. TOLENTINO : **Ano ang hinihintay mo?** *What are you waiting for?*

MELISSA : **Naghihintay po ako ng jeepney.** *I am waiting for the jeepney.*

MR. TOLENTINO : **Sumabay ka na sa akin. Pupunta rin ako sa Quezon City.** *Just ride with me. I'm also going to Quezon City.*

MELISSA : **Okay lang po. Malapit nang dumating ang jeepney.** *It's okay. The jeepney is arriving soon.*

MR. TOLENTINO : **Sige na, sumakay ka na sa kotse.** *Please get in the car.*

Now practice the dialogue.

> **CULTURE TIP (Repeating An Offer)** It is customary to offer someone a ride. However, it is not polite to accept the offer right away. Thus, the person being offered a ride will initially refuse by saying "**Okay lang po.**" (*It's okay.*)

VOCABULARY

First, study words related to transportation.

bus	*bus*	bisikleta	*bicycle*
estasyon ng bus	*bus station*	tren	*train*
		trak	*truck*
traysikel	*a motorcycle or a bicycle with a sidecar*	eroplano	*airplane*
		bangka	*small boat*
kotse	*car*	barko	*large ship*
taksi	*taxi*	milya	*miles*
LRT, MRT	short for *Light Rail Transit, Metro Rail Transit*	kilometro	*kilometers*

Next, study ways by which we travel.

biyahe	*travel*
pagbibiyahe	*traveling*
naglalakad	*walking*
nagbibisikleta	*riding a bicycle*
nagmamaneho	*driving*

GRAMMAR

Study how verbs used for transportation can be conjugated when the focus is on the actor (with **mag-** and **-um-** affixes), the object (with the **-in-** affix), or the direction (with **in-** and **-an** affixes) of the action.

The same conjugation rules you have previously learned still apply. Review the special rules in Chapter 15 for verbs ending in vowels or root words starting with **d**.

Actor Focus

Root	Completed	Incompleted	Contemplated
pumunta *go* or *come*	pumunta	pumupunta	pupunta
lakad *walk*	naglakad	naglalakad	maglalakad
maneho *drive*	nagmaneho	nagmamaneho	magmamaneho
hintay *wait*	naghintay	naghihintay	maghihintay
sakay *ride*	sumakay	sumasakay	sasakay
dating *arrive*	dumating	dumarating	darating

Read the following sentences to see how the verbs are used with the actor focus.

Naglakad si Ralph nang dalawang milya.	*Ralph walked two miles.*
Naghihintay si Melissa ng jeepney.	*Melissa is waiting for a jeepney.*
Dumarating na ang jeepney.	*The jeepney is already arriving.*
Sumakay si Mr. Tolentino ng kotse.	*Mr. Tolentino rode a car.*

Object focus

Root	Completed	Incompleted	Contemplated
lakad *walk*	nilakad	nilalakad	lalakarin
maneho *drive*	minaneho	minamaneho	imamaneho
hintay *wait*	hinintay	hinihintay	hihintayin
sakay *ride*	sinakay	isinasakay	isasakay

Read the following sentences to see how the verbs are used with the object focus. Note that the English translation is a literal translation to show the difference between the actor and object focus. The sentences could be logically translated in the same way as with the actor focus. **Dating** is not listed because it is not commonly used with the object focus.

Dalawang milya ang nilakad ni Ralph.	*Two miles is what Ralph walked.*
Hinihinintay niya ang jeepney.	*The jeepney is what she is waiting for.*
Isinasakay ni Mr. Tolentino si Melissa sa kanyang kotse.	*Melissa is being given a ride by Mr. Tolentino in his car.*

Directional Focus

Root	Completed	Incompleted	Contemplated
punta *go or come*	pinuntahan	pinupuntahan	pupuntahan
darating *arrive*	dinatnan	dinaratnan	daratnan
sakay *ride*	sinakyan	sinasakyan	sasakyan

Study the following sentences. As you have learned, the affixes **in-** and **-an** are used for directional focus. Additionally, they are used when the focus is on the location. This can best be illustrated in this chapter.

Unibersidad ang pupuntahan ni Melissa.	*The university is where Melissa will go.*
Kaklase niya ang dinatnan niya sa classroom.	*Her classmate is who was there when she arrived at the classroom.*
Tren ang sinasakyan ko.	*A train is what I ride.*

QUESTION AND ANSWER PRACTICE

Practice the following questions and answers. You will need to refer back to the previously introduced dialogues and sentence patterns to complete this exercise.

1. Question: **Naan ka pupunta?** *Where are you going?*

   Answer: **Pupunta ako sa unibersidad.** *I am going to the university.*

2. Question: **Ano ang hinihintay mo?** *What are you waiting for?*

   Answer: **Naghihintay ako ng jeepney.** *I am waiting for a jeepney.*

3. Question: **Saan pupunta si Melissa?**

   Answer: _____.

4. Question: **Ano ang hinihintay ni Melissa?**

   Answer: _____.

5. Question: _____?

   Answer: **Pupunta si Melissa sa unibersidad.**

6. Question: _____?

   Answer: **Naghihintay ng jeepney si Melissa.**

Where Are You Going?

Ralph is asking Sarah about her daily commute.

Study the following words, phrases, and sentences about transportation. Also, review what you have learned in Chapter 3 about **saan** (*where*, used only when there is a verb), and **nasaan** (*where*, used when there is no verb in the sentence).

Nasaan ang opisina mo?	Where + **ang** + office + your? *Where is your office?*

Nasa Makati ang opisina ko.	In + Makati + **ang** + office + my. *My office is in Makati.*
paano	*how*
Paano ka pumupunta sa opisina?	How + you + go + to + office? *How do you go to the office?*
Sumasakay ako ng taksi.	Ride + I + **ng** + taxi. *I ride a taxi.*
Saan ka naghihintay ng taksi?	Where + you + wait + **ng** + taxi? *Where do you wait for the taxi?*
sa harap	*in front of*
Sa tapat ng Megamall.	*Across from Megamall.*
magkano	*how much*
pamasahe	*fare*
magkano ang pamasahe	*how much is the fare*
mula	*from*
hanggang	*to*
mula sa Megamall hanggang sa Makati	*from Megamall to Makati*
Magkano ang pamasahe mula sa Megamall hanggang sa Makati?	How much + **ang** + fare + from Megamall + to + Makati? *How much is the fare from Megamall to Makati?*
singkuwenta	*fifty*
Singkuwenta pesos.	*Fifty pesos.*

 DIALOGUE B

RALPH : **Nasaan ang opisina mo?** *Where is your office?*
SARAH : **Nasa Makati ang opisina ko.** *My office is in Makati.*
RALPH : **Paano ka pumupunta sa opisina?** *How do you go to the office?*
SARAH : **Sumasakay ako ng taksi.** *I ride a taxi.*
RALPH : **Saan ka naghihintay ng taksi?** *Where do you wait for the taxi?*
SARAH : **Sa harap ng Megamall.** *In front of Megamall.*
RALPH : **Magkano ang pamasahe mula sa Megamall hanggang sa Makati?** *How much is the fare from Megamall to Makati?*
SARAH : **Singkuwenta pesos.** *50 pesos.*

Practice the dialogue.

QUESTION AND ANSWER PRACTICE

Practice the following questions and answers. You will need to refer back to the previously introduced dialogues and sentence patterns to complete this exercise.

1. Question: **Nasaan ang opisina mo?** *Where is your office?*

   Answer: **Nasa Makati ang opisina ko.** *My office is in Makati.*

2. Question: **Paano pumupunta sa opisina si Sarah?** *How does Sarah go to the office?*

   Answer: **Sumasakay ng taksi si Sarah.** *Sarah rides a taxi.*

3. Question: **Magkano ang pamasahe mula sa Megamall hanggang Makati?** *How much is the fare from Megamall to Makati?*

   Answer: **Singkuwenta pesos.** *Fifty pesos.*

4. Question: **Nasaan ang opisina ni Sarah?**

   Answer: _____.

5. Question: _____?

   Answer: **Sumasakay ng taksi si Sarah papuntang Makati.**

6. Question: _____?

   Answer: **Naghihintay si Sarah ng taksi.**

GRAMMAR

The words **pupunta** and **papunta** seem similar and can easily be confused. **Pupunta** (*will go/is going*) is a verb in the completed aspect, while **papunta** (formed from the affix **pa-** + the root word **punta**; *going to*) is part of an adjectival phrase. Here are some examples:

Pupunta si Melissa sa unibersidad.	Is going + **si** + Melissa + to + university. *Melissa is going to the university.*
papunta	*going*
Pupunta ako sa meeting.	Will go + I + to + meeting. *I will go to the meeting.*
na	used to mean *that*

na papunta sa airport	that + going + to + airport *that is going to the airport*
Sumasakay si Ralph ng bus na papunta sa airport.	Riding + **si** + Ralph + **ng** + bus + that + going + to +airport. *Ralph is catching a bus going to the airport.*

Note that when the sentence is translated to natural in English, the relative pronoun *that* (**na**) is dropped. Similarly, most people opt to drop **na** (*that*) in Tagalog, resulting in the following sentence.

Sumasakay si Ralph ng bus papunta sa airport.	Riding + **si** + Ralph + **ng** + going + to + airport. *Ralph is catching a bus going to the airport.*

How do I get there?

Ralph needs to go to the airport. Melissa is asking him how he will get there. Read and then practice the following dialogue.

First, here are some common places in Metro Manila:

EDSA	acronym for **E**pifanio **d**e los **S**antos **A**venue; the long avenue that stretches from north to south of Metro Manila
NAIA	acronym for **N**inoy **A**quino **I**nternational **A**irport, the main international airport in Metro Manila
Megamall	a large landmark mall in EDSA

Now, study how the questions and answers are constructed.

Paano ka pupunta sa airport?	How + you + will go + to + airport? *How will you go to the airport?*
Sasakay ako ng bus.	Will ride + I + **ng** + bus. *I will ride a bus.*
Saan ka sasakay ng bus?	Where + you + will ride + **ng** + bus? *Where will you catch the bus?*
Sasakay ako ng bus sa EDSA.	Will ride + I + **ng** + bus + in + EDSA. *I will catch the bus in EDSA.*
alin	*which*
aling (contraction of **alin + na**)	*which*
aling bus	*which bus*

Aling bus ang sasakyan mo?	Which + bus + **ang** + will ride + you? *Which bus will you catch?*
papunta	*going to*
papunta sa NAIA	*going to NAIA*
na	*that*
bus na papunta sa NAIA	*bus that is going to NAIA*
Sasakay ako ng bus na papunta sa NAIA.	Will ride + I + **ng** + bus + that + going + to + NAIA. *I will catch the bus going to NAIA.*
Magkano ang pamasahe papunta sa NAIA?	How much + **ang** + fare + going + to + NAIA? *How much is the fare going to NAIA?*

DIALOGUE C

MELISSA : **Paano ka pupunta sa airport?** *How will you go to the airport?*

RALPH : **Sasakay ako ng bus.** *I will ride a bus.*

MELISSA : **Saan ka sasakay ng bus?** *Where will you catch the bus?*

RALPH : **Sasakay ako ng bus sa EDSA.** *I will catch the bus in EDSA.*

MELISSA : **Aling bus ang sasakyan mo?** *Which bus will you catch?*

RALPH : **Sasakay ako ng bus na papunta sa NAIA.** *I will catch the bus going to NAIA.*

MELISSA : **Magkano ang pamasahe papunta sa NAIA?** *How much is the fare to NAIA?*

RALPH : **Otsenta pesos ang pamasahe ko.** *The fare is eighty pesos.*

> **VOCABULARY AND CULTURE TIP** Filipinos are also very fond of using acronyms for places such as EDSA and NAIA. You will also encounter acronyms for names or nicknames.

QUESTION AND ANSWER PRACTICE

Now, let us practice some questions and answers using the dialogues, vocabulary and conjugations we previously learned.

1. Question: **Paano ka pupunta sa airport?**
   How will you go to the airport?

   Answer: **Sasakay ako ng bus.** *I will ride the bus.*

2. Question: **Saan ka sasakay ng bus?** *Where will you catch the bus?*

   Answer: **Sasakay ako ng bus sa EDSA.** *I will catch the bus in EDSA.*

3. Question: **Aling bus ang sasakyan mo?** *Which bus will you ride?*

   Answer: **Sasakay ako ng bus papunta sa NAIA.** *I will ride the bus going to NAIA.*

4. Question: **Magkano ang pamasahe papunta sa NAIA?** *How much is the fare going to NAIA?*

   Answer: **Otsenta pesos ang pamasahe ko.** *The fare is eighty pesos.*

5. Question: _____?

   Answer: **Sasakay ako ng taksi.**

6. Question: **Saan ka sasakay ng taksi?**

   Answer: _____.

7. Question: **Aling taksi ang sasakyan mo, ang taksing papunta sa NAIA, O ang taksing papunta sa Clark Airport?**

   Answer: _____.

   _____.

8. Question: _____?

   Answer: **Dos siyentos pesos ang pamasahe ko.**

DIALOGUE PRACTICE

Practice what you have just learned. Create dialogues according to the following situations.

Situation 1 Ralph is waiting for a taxi in front of his office building. He is on his way to a bus station in Pasay City. His co-worker sees him and offers him a ride. He declines but the co-worker insists. Ralph tells his co-worker that he will take the Calamba bus at the station.

Co-worker : **Saan ka pupunta?**

Ralph : _____.

Co-worker : **Ano ang hinihintay mo?**

Ralph : _____.

Co-worker : **Anong bus ang sasakyan mo sa estasyon ng bus?**

RALPH : _____.

_____.

Situation 2 Sarah is in her office preparing to leave. Her co-worker asks her how she is going home. She tells him that she will take the train. She asks him how he goes to work and he tells her that he drives. Remember that the word for *go home*, as you have learned in Chapter 12, is **uwi**.

CO-WORKER : **Uuwi ka na ba?**

SARAH : _____.

CO-WORKER : **Paano ka umuuwi sa bahay mo?**

SARAH : _____. **Ikaw, paano ka pumupunta sa trabaho?**

CO-WORKER : _____.

SUMMING UP

Let us review what we have just learned in Chapter 17. Fill in the blanks with the new verbs and nouns you can use when talking about transportation.

_____ si Melissa ng jeepney. _____ siya

sa unibersidad. Si Mr. Tolentino ay _____ ng kotse.

_____ na ang jeepney.

Nasa Makati ang _____ ni Sarah. _____ ng

taksi si Sarah. Singkuwenta pesos ang _____ ni Sarah

_____ MegaMall _____ sa Makati.

_____ si Ralph sa airport. _____ siya ng bus

_____ sa EDSA. Otsenta pesos ang _____

papuntang NAIA.

CHAPTER 18

What time does the bus leave?
Anong oras umaalis ang bus?

In this chapter, review words for time, money, and transportation and learn to conjugate new words related to travel.

Ralph is at the bus station, buying a ticket for a bus to Baguio City.

Going Out of Town

Review words and phrases to tell the time, and study the following new words, phrases, and sentences used when travelling.

Anong oras na po?	What + **na** + time + already + **po?** *What time is it?*
puwedeng sumakay	*can ride, can take*
papuntang (contraction of **papunta** + **na**)	*going to*
bus na papuntang Baguio City	*bus going to Baguio City*
Saan po ako puwedeng sumakay ng bus na papuntang Baguio City?	Where + **po** + I + can ride + **ng** + bus + that + going + to + Baguio City? *Where can I take a bus going to Baguio City?*
doon	*over there*
karatula	*sign*
karatula na	*sign that is*
karatula na Baguio	*sign that is Baguio*
karatulang (contraction **karatula** + **na**) **Baguio**	*sign that is Baguio*
na may karatulang "Baguio"	that + has + sign + Baguio *with the sign (saying) Baguio*

Sumakay ka sa bus na may karatulang "Baguio."	Ride + you + in + bus + that + has + sign + that + is + Baguio. *Take the bus with the sign (saying) Baguio.*
aalis	*leave*
Anong oras po aalis ang bus?	What time + **po** + leave + **ang** + bus? *What time will the bus leave?*
alas-diyes y medya	*10:30*
Alas diyes y medya aalis ang bus.	10:30 + leave + **ang** + bus. *The bus will leave at 10:30.*
darating	*arrive*
Anong oras po darating ang bus sa Baguio City?	What time + **po** + arrive + **ang** + bus + in + Baguio City? *What time will the bus arrive in Baguio City?*
bandang	*around*
Bandang alas-tres ng madaling araw.	*Around three o'clock in the early morning.*
bababa	*getting off/will get off*
Saan po kayo bababa?	Where + **po** + you + getting off? *Where are you getting off?*
tapat	*across from*
palengke	*market*
na lang	*just*
sa tapat ng palengke	*across from the market*
Sa tapat na lang ng palengke ng Baguio City.	At + across from + just + of + market of + Baguio City. *Just across from the Baguio City market.*

🔘 **DIALOGUE A**

RALPH : Excuse me, anong oras na po? *Excuse me, what time is it?*

BABAE : Alas-nuwebe po ng gabi. *It's nine o'clock at night.*

RALPH : Salamat po. Saan po ako puwedeng sumakay ng bus na papuntang Baguio City? *Thank you. Where can I catch the bus going to Baguio City?*

BABAE : Doon. Sumakay ka sa bus na may karatulang "Baguio." *Over there. Take the bus with the sign (saying) "Baguio."*

RALPH	: Anong oras po aalis ang bus? *What time will the bus leave?*
BABAE	: Alas-diyes y medya aalis ang bus. *The bus is leaving at 10:30.*
MR. TOLENTINO	: Anong oras po darating ang bus sa Baguio City? *What time will the bus arrive in Baguio City?*
BABAE	: Bandang alas-tres ng madaling-araw. Saan po kayo bababa? *Around three o'clock in the early morning. Where are you getting off?*
MR. TOLENTINO	: Sa tapat na lang ng palengke ng Baguio City. *Just across from the Baguio City Market.*

Now practice the dialogue.

VOCABULARY

The following words are useful for talking about transportation and travel.

harap/harapan	*in front of*
likod/likuran	*behind, at the back of*
biyahe	*trip*
kanan	*right*
kaliwa	*left*
direksiyon	*direction*
hilaga	*north*
timog	*south*
silangan	*east*
kanluran	*south*

GRAMMAR

Let us study three verbs that were introduced in the dialogue, and learn their conjugation with actor focus.

Root	Completed	Incompleted	Contemplated
alis *leave*	umalis	umaalis	aalis
baba *get off/go down*	bumaba	bumababa	bababa
biyahe *take a trip*	nagbiyahe	nagbibiyahe	magbibiyahe

Read the following sentences to see how the verbs are used with the actor focus.

Magbibiyahe si Ralph papuntang hilaga.	*Ralph will take a trip going north.*
Aalis si Ralph papuntang Baguio City mamayang gabi.	*Ralph is leaving for Baguio City later tonight.*
Bababa si Ralph sa tapat ng palengke ng Baguio City.	*Ralph is getting off in front of the Baguio City market.*
Darating ang bus sa Baguio City ng bandang alas-tres ng madaling araw.	*The bus will arrive in Baguio City at around three o'clock in the early morning.*
Sumakay si Ralph sa bus na may karatulang "Baguio."	*Ralph took the bus with the sign (saying) "Baguio."*

QUESTION AND ANSWER PRACTICE

First answer the following questions about the dialogue you have just read.

1. Question: **Saan** _____ **si Ralph papuntang** _____?

   Answer: **Sasakay si Ralph sa** _____ **na may** _____ **"Baguio."**

2. Question: **Anong oras aalis ang bus papuntang Baguio City?**

   Answer: _____.

3. Question: **Anong oras darating ang bus sa Baguio City?**

   Answer: _____.

4. Question: _____?

   Answer: **Bababa si Ralph sa** _____.

Now, answer these questions based on the following information: You are taking a trip going south. The bus is leaving Manila at 12:00 p.m. and arriving Lipa City at around 3 p.m. You are getting off across from the Lipa market.

Refer to the previous dialogue and new vocabulary words, as well as the vocabulary words on time found in Lesson 11.

1. Question: **Saan ka magbibiyahe?**

   Answer: _____.

2. Question: **Anong oras aalis ang bus sa Manila?**

   Answer: (12:00 P.M.) _____.

3. Question: **Anong oras darating ang bus sa Lipa City?**

   Answer: (3:00 P.M.) _____.

4. Question: **Saan ka bababa?**

   Answer: _____.

> **CULTURE TIP (Departure Times)** In some areas in the countryside, there are no set departure times for buses and jeepneys in transportation terminals. Usually, the bus or jeepney leaves when it is full. Patience is the key.

Buying a Bus Ticket

Ralph is taking another trip to Baguio City. Study this conversation to practice time, numbers, and vocabulary related to shopping.

pabili	*to buy, would like to buy*
tiket	*ticket*
Pabili po ng tiket papuntang Baguio City.	Would like to buy + **po** + **ng** + ticket + going + to + Baguio City.
	I would like to buy a bus ticket going to Baguio City.
gustong umalis	*want to leave*
Anong oras po ninyo gustong umalis?	What time + **po** + you + want + to leave?
	What time do you want to leave?
ilan	*how many*
Ilang tiket po ang gusto ninyo?	How many + ticket + **po** + **ang** + want + you?
	How many tickets do you want?
magkano	*how much*
Magkano ang isang tiket?	How much + **ang** + one + ticket?
	How much is a ticket?

Dalawang daang piso po.	*200 pesos.*
bakit	*why*
mahal	*expensive*
Bakit po mahal ang tiket?	Why + **po** + expensive + **ang** + ticket? *Why is the ticket so expensive?*
kasi/dahil	*because*
Kasi naka-aircon po ang bus.	Because + air conditioned + **po** + **ang** + bus. *Because the bus is air conditioned.*
Ah, ganoon ba?	*Is that so?*

 DIALOGUE B

Read the dialogue below.

RALPH   : **Pabili po ng tiket papuntang Baguio City.** *I want to buy a ticket going to Baguio City.*

TICKET AGENT : **Anong oras po ninyo gustong umalis?** *What time do you want to leave?*

RALPH   : **Alas-diyes y medya po.** *At 10:30.*

TICKET AGENT	:	**Ilang tiket po ang gusto ninyo?** *How many tickets do you want?*
RALPH	:	**Isa lang po. Magkano po ang isang tiket?** *Just one. How much is a ticket?*
TICKET AGENT	:	**Dalawang daang piso po.** *200 pesos.*
RALPH	:	**Heto po ang dalawang daang piso. Bakit po mahal ang tiket?** *Here is the 200 pesos. Why is the ticket so expensive?*
TICKET AGENT	:	**Kasi naka-aircon po ang bus.** *Because the bus is air conditioned.*
RALPH	:	**Ah, ganoon ba? Maraming salamat.** *Oh, is that so? Thank you very much.*

Then, practice this dialogue by using your own information.

VOCABULARY

Study the following adjectives and adverbs as they are used in sentences.

maaga	*early*
pinakamaaga	*earliest*
Gusto kong sumakay sa pinakamaagang bus.	*I want to take the earliest bus.*
huli (pronounced with accent on the last syllable)	*late* (aslo, *last*)
pinakahuli	*very last*
Huli ang bus.	*The bus is late.*
Gusto kong sumakay sa pinakahuling bus.	*I want to takw the very last bus.*
mabagal	*slow*
mabilis	*fast*

QUESTION AND ANSWER PRACTICE

Practice answering the questions below. Use what you have learned in the previous chapters, dialogues, and exercises.

1. Question: **Saan pupunta si Ralph?**

   Answer: _____.

2. Question: **Anong oras aalis ang bus na sasakyan ni Ralph?**

   Answer: _____.

3. Question: **Ilang tiket ang binili niya?**

   Answer: _____.

4. Question: **Magkano ang isang tiket papuntang Baguio City?**

   Answer: _____.

DIALOGUE PRACTICE

Create dialogues using the information provided. Practice the vocabulary words you learned.

Situation 1 You are buying two bus tickets to go to Pampanga with your friend. You want to take the earliest bus. Each ticket costs eight pesos. The tickets are expensive because the bus is fast (has fewer stops).

You   : _____ **ho ng bus tiket** _____.

Ticket Agent : _____ **tiket ho ang** _____?

You   : _____.

Ticket Agent : **Anong oras po ninyo gustong umalis?**

You   : _____.

_____ **po ang isang tiket?**

Ticket Agent : _____.

You   : **Bakit po mahal ang tiket?**

Ticket Agent : _____.

Situation 2 You are buying five bus tickets for a trip with your friends to go north to Banuae. You want to take the very last bus. The bus leaves at 11:45 in the evening. The fare is usually two hundred and fifty pesos, but is cheaper because you can get a group discount.

You   : _____.

Ticket Agent : _____ **tiket ho ang** _____?

You   : _____.

Ticket Agent : **Anong oras** _____?

You   : _____.

              Magkano po _____?

Ticket Agent : **Dalawang daan at tatlumpung piso na lang.**

You   : **Bakit po** _____?

Ticket Agent : _____.

SUMMING UP

Let us try to sum up what you have learned in Chapter 18.

Write a few sentences about your experience of going to the bus station, asking for information, and buying a ticket. Use the new vocabulary, verbs, and adjectives you have learned so far.

_____

_____

_____

_____

_____

_____

_____

_____

CHAPTER 19

Can you take me to the shopping mall?
Puwede n'yo ba akong dalhin sa shopping mall?

In this chapter, learn about how to give directions. For grammar, study reported speech and how to form complex sentences.

Ralph is taking a taxi to the shopping mall, but the taxi driver is not sure how to get there.

Taxi!

Study the following words, phrases, and sentences about giving directions.

dala	*take, bring* (root word)
dalhin	*take* (infinitive form)
puwede niyo ba akong dalhin	can + you + **ba** + me + **na** + take *can you take me*
Puwede niyo ba akong dalhin sa shopping mall?	Can + you + **ba** + me + **na** + take + to + shopping mall? *Can you take me to the shopping mall?*
Alin pong mall?	Which + **po** + **na** + mall? *Which mall?*
pinakamalapit na shopping mall	*closest/nearest shopping mall*
Sa pinakamalapit na shopping mall sa Quezon City.	To + closest + **na** + shopping mall + in + Quezon City. *To the nearest shopping mall in Quezon City.*
alam	*know*
Alam niyo ba?	Know + you + **ba**? *Do you know?*
kung paano pumunta roon	if + how + go + there *how to go there*

Alam niyo ba kung paano pumunta roon?	Know + how + **ba** + if + how + go + there? *Do you know how to get there?*
dumiretso	*go straight*
Dumiretso kayo papuntang EDSA.	Go straight + you + going to + EDSA. *Go straight heading towards EDSA.*
pagkatapos	*then*
kumanan	*turn right, make a right*
Pagkatapos, kumanan kayo sa EDSA.	Then + make a right + you + on + EDSA. *Then, make a right turn on EDSA.*
lumampas	*go past*
ilaw	*light, traffic light*
Lumampas kayo ng limang ilaw-trapiko.	Go past + you + **ng** + five + traffic lights. *Go past five traffic lights.*
nasa kanan	*on your right*
Nasa kanan ang mall.	On + right + **ang** + mall. *The mall will be on the right.*

Read the dialogue below.

DIALOGUE A

RALPH   : **Puwede niyo ba akong dalhin sa shopping mall?**
                Can you take me to the shopping mall?

TAXI DRIVER : **Alin pong mall?** *Which mall?*

RALPH   : **Sa pinakamalapit na shopping mall sa Quezon City.**
                The nearest mall in Quezon City.

TAXI DRIVER : **Alam niyo ba kung paano po pumunta roon?**
                Do you know how to get there?

RALPH   : **Alam ko ho. Dumiretso po kayo papuntang EDSA.**
                Pagkatapos, kumanan kayo sa EDSA. Dumiretso kayo.
                Lumampas kayo ng limang ilaw-trapiko. Nasa kanan
                ang mall. *I do. Go straight, heading towards EDSA. Then,*
                make a right turn on EDSA, and keep straight. Next, pass 5
                traffic lights. The mall will be on the right.

> **VOCABULARY TIP (Direction Words)** When giving directions in Tagalog, direction words can be transformed into verbs. For example, the direction words **kanan** (*right*), **kaliwa** (*left*), **diretso** (*straight*), **hinto** (*stop*), **lampas** (*past*), and **hinto** (*stop*) can be transformed into verbs by adding the affix **um-** to them.

VOCABULARY

Study other words, phrases and sentences that can be used to ask and give directions.

kalye	*street*
iskinita	*alley*
daan	*road* (also means *pass*)
kalsada	*road*
Kumaliwa ka sa kalyeng iyan.	*Turn left on that street.*
Dumiretso ka sa daang ito.	*Go straight on this road.*
Umikot ka sa Rotonda.	*Go around the Rotonda.*
Bumalik ka.	*Go back.*
Huminto ka.	*Stop.*
Kumanan ka papuntang Maginhawa Street.	*Turn right to go on Maginhawa Street.*
Kumaliwa ka sa pangatlong kanto.	*Turn left on the third corner.*
Lumampas ka ng apat na ilaw-trapiko.	*Go pass four traffic lights.*
mula/galing	*from*
mula/galing sa unibersidad	*from the university*
Paano pumunta sa mall mula sa unibersidad?	How + go + mall + from + university? *How can I go to the mall from the university?*
Galing sa unibersidad, paano pumunta sa mall?	From + at + university + how + go + to + mall *From the university, how can I go to the mall?*

GRAMMAR

Forming Complex Sentences

First, let us study sentences that start with the phrase, **Alam mo ba?** (*Do you know?*). To attach a clause starting with a question word, for example, **paano** (*how*), we use the word **kung** (*if*).

Study the sentence structure and then the examples below.

Do you know + **kung** + question word + phrase?
Alam mo ba + kung + paano + pumunta sa unibersidad?

Question: **Alam mo ba kung paano pumunta sa University of the Philippines?** *Do you know how to go to the University of the Philippines?*

Answer: **Alam ko kung paano pumunta sa University of the Philippines.** *I know how to go to the University of the Philippines.*

Question: **Alam mo ba kung nasaan ang shopping mall?** *Do you know where the shopping mall is?*

Answer: **Hindi ko alam kung nasaan ang shopping mall.** *I don't know where the shopping mall is.*

Sentences starting with "galing sa/mula sa (from)"

Next, let us study sentences using phrases that start with **galing sa** or **mula sa** (*from*). These words have exactly the same meaning, and are interchangeable.

Question: **Paano pumunta sa sinehan?** *How does one get to the movie theater?*

Answer: **Galing sa EDSA papuntang Monumento, nasa kanan ang sinehan.** *The movie theater is on the right from EDSA to Monumento.*

Question: **Paano pumunta sa Fairview mula sa Philcoa?** *How can I get to Fairview from Philcoa?*

Answer: **Mula sa Philcoa, dumiretso po kayo sa Commonwealth Avenue. Nasa bandang dulo ng highway na ito ang Fairview.** *Go straight on Commonwealth Avenue from Philcoa. Fairview is somewhere around the end of this road, close to Batasan.*

DIALOGUE PRACTICE

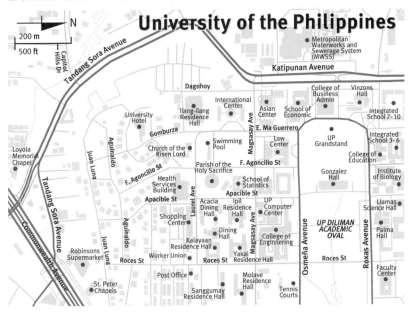

Practice asking and giving directions using the above map. Write your own questions based on the map.

1. Question: **Paano ako pupunta sa Kalayaan Residence Hall mula sa International Center?**

   Answer: **Mula sa UP Arcade, _____ po kayo sa Laurel Avenue. Tapos, kumaliwa po kayo sa _____.**

   Nasa kaliwang kanto po ang Kalayaan Residence Hall.

2. Question: **Paano ako pupunta sa Church of the Risen Lord mula sa UP Computer Center?**

   Answer: **_____ ka sa Magsaysay Avenue.**

   _____ ka sa Agoncillo Street

   _____ ka sa _____.

   Nasa _____ mo ang Church of the Risen Lord.

3. Question: **Paano ako pupunta sa UP International Center mula sa Faculty Center?**

   Answer: _____

   _____.

4. Question: _____?

   Answer: _____

   _____.

5. Question: _____?

   Answer: _____

   _____.

CULTURE NOTE (On the Street) When Filipinos see each other on the street, they usually ask **Kumusta ka?** (*How are you?*), followed by **Saan ka pupunta?** (*Where are you going?*), **Saan ka galing?** (*Where did you come from?*), and **Kumain ka na ba?** (*Have you eaten?*). This questioning should not be misconstrued as being nosey. It should instead be viewed as concern for one's well being.

Change of Plans

Melissa and Sarah have been invited to Mr. Tolentino's birthday party. Ralph has offered to pick them up, but he is coming from a meeting and might be late. They are discussing if it would be better to take a taxi instead.

Study the following words, phrases, and sentences to learn about reported speech.

sundo	*fetch, pick up*
susunduin	*is picking up, will pick up*
Susunduin ba tayo ni Ralph?	Pick up + **ba** + us + **ni** Ralph?
	Will Ralph pick us up?
pero	*but*
mahuhuli	*will be late*
raw/daw	used to mean *he/she said*
Oo, pero mahuhuli raw siya.	Yes, + but + will be late + said + he
	Yes, but he said he would be late.
Bakit	*Why?*

manggagaling	*coming from*
opisina	*office*
Manggaling siya sa opisina.	Coming from + he + at + office. *He is coming from the office.*
hanggang	*until*
May meeting siya hanggang alas siyete y medya ng gabi.	Has + meeting + he + until + seven+ thirty + in + evening. *He has a meeting until seven thirty in the evening.*
magtaksi	*take a taxi*
kaya	*what if, how about*
Magtaksi na lang kaya tayo?	Take a taxi + just + how about + we? *How about just taking a cab?*
sasabihin	*will say, will tell*
sasabihin ko sa kanya	*will tell him*
Sige, sasabihin ko sa kanya.	*Okay, I will tell him.*

DIALOGUE B

SARAH : **Susunduin ba tayo ni Ralph?** *Will Ralph pick us up?*

MELISSA : **Oo, pero mahuhuli raw siya.** *Yes, but he said he would be late.*

SARAH : **Bakit?** *Why?*

MELISSA : **Manggagaling siya sa opisina. May meeting siya hanggang alas-siyete y medya ng gabi.** *He is coming from the office. He has a meeting until 7:30 p.m.*

SARAH : **Magtaksi na lang kaya tayo?** *How about just taking a cab?*

MELISSA : **Sige, sasabihin ko sa kanya.** *Okay, I'll tell him.*

GRAMMAR

Reported Speech

The words **daw** and **raw** are used for reported speech. In spoken Tagalog, these two words can be interchanged. However, in written Tagalog, **daw** is used when the preceding word ends in a consonant, while **raw** is used when the preceding word ends in a vowel.

To repeat what another person has said, put the word **daw** or **raw** before the name of the person or the pronoun.

 **DIALOGUE C**

RALPH : **Mahuhuli ako.** *I will be late.*

SARAH : **Ano ang sabi ni Ralph?** *What did Ralph say?*

MELISSA : **Mahuhuli raw si Ralph.** *Ralph said he will be late.*

Or, **Mahuhuli raw siya.** *He said he will be late.*

RALPH : **Manggagaling ako sa opisina.** *I am coming from the office.*

MELISSA : **Manggagaling daw si Ralph sa opisina.** *Ralph said he was coming from the office.*

Making Suggestions

To make a suggestion, use the word **kaya** (*how about?*). Put **kaya** immediately after the verb or a verbal phrase. For example.

Magtaksi kaya tayo?	Take a taxi + how about + we? *How about taking a taxi?*
Magtaksi na lang kaya tayo?	Take a taxi + just + how about + we? *How about just taking a taxi?*
Kumanan kaya tayo?	Turning right + how about + we? *How about turning right?*

DIALOGUE PRACTICE

Practice the grammar points you have just learned. Create dialogues based on the following situations.

Situation 1 You and your sister Jill are are going to Suzette's house. Suzette had told you to come at 7 p.m. Your sister wants to take a cab. You suggest taking a train to avoid the traffic.

JILL : **Ano ang sabi ni Suzette?**

YOU : _____.

JILL : **Sumakay tayo ng** _____.

YOU : **May traffic.** _____?

JILL : **Sige.**

Situation 2 Ralph and Mr. Tolentino are waiting for a colleague, Mr. Baquiran. They are having a lunch meeting at a restaurant. Mr. Baquiran had told Ralph that he is coming from Tagaytay and might be late. Mr. Tolentino suggests that they order and start eating.

Mr. Tolentino : **Ano ang sabi ni Mr. Baquiran?**

Ralph : _____.

Mr. Tolentino : **Saan siya manggagaling?**

Ralph : _____.

Mr. Tolentino : _____?

Ralph : **Sige.**

SUMMING UP

In this chapter, we have focused on asking and giving directions, command verbs, and locations, along with words for reported speech and giving suggestions.

Let us sum up the chapter by writing a paragraph giving directions from one place to another (for example, from your apartment to the library, from the bus stop to your place of work).

_____

_____

_____

_____

_____

_____

CHAPTER 20

What shall I wear to the party?

Ano ang isusuot ko sa party?

In this chapter, learn more adjectives to describe clothing. For grammar, study the use of **na** as a relative pronoun. Also, learn more greetings and compliments.

Sarah is shopping for a blouse at Marconi's Fashion House for the party. She is a **mamimili** (*shopper*) and the salesperson is a **tindera**. Let us first study words and phrases that she can use in shopping (**pamimili**):

Shopping for a Blouse

magkano	*how much*
blusa	blouse
Magkano ho ang blusang ito?	How much + **ho** + **ang** blouse + **na** + this? *How much does this blouse cost?*
limang daan	*five hundred*
Limang daang piso ho.	Five hundred + pesos + **ho**. *Five hundred pesos.*
bili	*buy* (root word)
bibilhin	*will buy*
Bibilhin ko na ho.	Will buy + I + already + **ho**. *I will buy it.*
sanlibo	*one thousand*
Heto ho ang sanlibong piso.	Here + **ho** + **ang** + one thousand pesos. *Here is one thousand pesos.*
sukli	*change*
Heto ho ang sukli niyo.	Here + **ho** + **ang** + change + your. *Here is your change.*

Study this dialogue. Note that they are using the honorific word **ho**, because they are strangers.

SARAH : **Magkano ho ang blusang ito?** *How much does this blouse cost?*
TINDERA : **Limang daang piso ho.** *It is five hundred pesos.*
SARAH : **Bibilhin ko na ho. Heto ho ang sanlibong piso.**
I will buy it. Here is one thousand pesos.
TINDERA : **Heto ho ang sukli ninyo.** *Here is your change.*

Now practice the dialogue.

VOCABULARY

Let us learn the names of other pieces of clothing and accessories which you may see in a fashion store.

damit	*clothing* (also refers to a woman's one-piece dress)
bestida	*dress* (refers only to a woman's one-piece dress)
palda	*skirt*
pantalon	*pants*
maong	*denim pants*
shorts	*shorts*
t-shirt	*t-shirt*
polo shirt/polo	*shirt*
shorts	*shorts*
sumbrero	*hat*
sinturon	*belt*
sapatos	*shoes*
sandalyas	*sandals*

Now practice the dialogue again, this time substituting a new word you have learned.

QUESTION AND ANSWER PRACTICE

Practice the conjugations of **bili** (*buy*) and review the vocabulary words you have just learned. Translate the words provided and use them in your sentences.

1. Question: **Ano ang gusto mong bilhin?**

   Answer (*hat*): _____.

2. Question: **Sino ang bumili ng blusa?**

   Answer (*Melissa*): _____.

3. Question: **Ano ang binili ni Ralph?**

   Answer (*maong*): _____.

4. Question(*shoes*): **Sino ang** _____?

   Answer: **Si Sarah ang bumibili ng sapatos.**

5. Question: **Ano ang bibilhin ni Mr. Tolentino?**

   Answer (*shirt*): _____.

GRAMMAR AND PRACTICE

Let us review some of the words and phrases you have learned in previous chapters, such as the helping verb **gusto** (*want*), the infinitive form of the verb **bumili** (*buy*), and colors. At the same time, let us also learn new verbs and adjectival phrases that will help describe clothing. Remember, Filipinos sometimes use English words to describe clothing because there are no indigenous words, or the English terms are more popular.

gusto ko hong bumili	*I want to buy*
Gusto ko hong bumili **ng blusa.**	Want + I + **ho** + **na** + buy + **ng** + blouse. *I want to buy a blouse.*
klaseng blusa	*kind of blouse*
Ano hong klaseng blusa?	What + **ho** + **na** + kind + **na** + blouse

Use of "na" as relative pronoun

In Tagalog, the word **na** (used as the relative pronoun *that*) is essential in forming adjectival phrases. Study the following examples.

blusa na may kuwelyo	blouse + that + has + collar *a blouse that has a collar*

kuwelyo na pabilog	collar + that + round. *a round collar*
V ang neckline	V + **ang** + neckline *V-neck*
blusa na V ang neckline	blouse + that + V + **ang** + neckline *a blouse with a V-neck*
blusa na walang kuwelyo	blouse + that + no + **na** + collar *a blouse with no collar*
walang manggas/sleeveless	*sleeveless*
blusa na walang manggas	blouse + that + no + **na** + sleeves *a sleeveless blouse*
maiksi ang manggas	*short sleeves*
polo na maiksi ang manggas	polo + that + short + **ang** + sleeves *short-sleeved shirt*
polo na mabaha ang	shirt + that + long + **ang** + sleeves **manggas** *a long-sleeved shirt*

Practice modals or helping verbs and new adjectival phrases by answering the following questions using the prompts provided.

1. Question: **Ano ang gusto mong bilhin?**

   Answer (*a sleeveless blouse*): _____.

2. Question: **Anong klaseng blusa ang gusto mong bilhin?**

   Answer (*blouse with a round collar*): _____.

3. Question: **Anong klaseng polo ang gusto mong bilhin?**

   Answer (*a long-sleeved shirt*): _____.

4. Question: **Anong klaseng bestida ang gusto mong bilhin?**

   Answer (dress with a V neckline): _____.

5. Question: **Ano ang gusto mong bilhin?**

   Answer (*shirt with short sleeves*): _____.

Choosing a Dress

Melissa is buying a dress to wear. She will be going to the Christmas party with Sarah. Study the following words, phrases, and sentences to prepare for the dialogue. Also review the words for colors you learned earlier.

klase	*kind*
anong klaseng bestida	what + **na** + kind + **na** + blouse
	what kind of blouse
hanap	*look* (root word)
hinahanap	*looking for*
Ano hong klaseng blusa ang hinahanap niyo?	What + **ho** + **na** + kind + **na** + blouse + **ang** + looking + you?
	What kind of blouse are you looking for?
iyon	*that*
Iyon hong sleeveless na bestida.	That + **ho** + **na** + sleeveless + **na** + dress.
	A sleeveless dress.
Heto ho.	*Here it is.*
ito	*this* (demonstrative subject pronoun)
nito	*this* (demonstrative object pronoun)
nito sa asul	*this in blue*
Mayroon ho ba kayo nito sa asul?	Have + **ho** + **ba** + you + this + in blue?
	Do you have this in blue?

DIALOGUE B

MELISSA : **Gusto ko hong bumili ng bestida.** *I want to buy a dress.*

TINDERA : **Ano hong klaseng bestida ang hinahanap niyo?**
What kind of dress are you looking for?

MELISSA : **Iyon hong sleeveless na bestida.** *A sleeveless dress*

TINDERA : **Heto ho.** *Here it is.*

MELISSA : **Mayroon ho ba kayo nito sa asul?** *Do you have this in blue?*

TINDERA : **Heto ho.** *Here it is.*

VOCABULARY

Study these words, and then practice the dialogue again, using your own ideas.

tela	*fabric/cloth*
gawa sa/yari sa	*made of*
gawa sa/yari sa	*made in*
seda/sutla	*silk*
cotton	*cotton*
lana	*wool*

tabas	shape, cut, style
sandali lang	one moment
Aalamin ko ho.	I will find out.
Titingnan ko ho.	I will look.
Mayroon ba kayo nito sa …?	Do you have this in …?

DIALOGUE PRACTICE

Study the following dialogues about shopping. Then, review the words you have just learned. Practice them to ask and answer similar questions. Translate the words provided in parenthesis and use them in formulating your questions and answers.

Exchange 1

MELISSA : **Saan ho gawa ito?** *Where is this made?*
TINDERA : **Sa Tsina ho.** *In China.*

Exchange 2

MELISSA : **Ano ho ang telang ito?** *What is this fabric?*
TINDERA : **Gawa ang blusang ito sa seda.** *This is made of silk.*

Exchange 3

MELISSA : **Mayroon ho ba kayong pula nito?** *Do you have this in red?*
TINDERA : **Aalamin ko ho. Sandali lang.** *I will find out. One moment.*

1. Question: **Saan gawa ang bestidang ito?**

   Answer (*Canada*): _____.

2. Question: **Ano ho ang telang ito?**

   Answer (*jacket*): _____ ang jacket na ito _____.

3. Question (*to a salesperson*): **Mayroon ho ba kayong asul nito?**

   Answer (*to a customer*): _____.

4. Question (*made in*): _____?

   Answer: **Gawa ho ito sa Japan.**

5. Question (*cloth*): _____?

   Answer: **Gawa ho ang pantalong ito sa cotton.**

6. Question (*green*): _____?

   Answer: **Aalamin ko ho. Sandali lang.**

Practice the exchanges you have just learned. Change the circumstances—look for a different color, fabric, or style—to get accustomed to the phrases and sentences you can use while shopping for clothes.

Now, let's move on to something that's also useful—bargaining! Bargaining is usually done in farmers' markets (**tiangge**) or wet markets (**palengke**, called as such because these markets also sell fish which are constantly being cleaned, making the floor wet). These markets sell everything from produce to household wares and clothes. However, in small stores found in shopping malls, you may also want to try your luck in bargaining.

GRAMMAR

In the dialogue earlier, you learned the use of the demonstrative pronoun **nito** (*this*).

Mayroon ho ba kayo nito sa asul? *Do you have this in blue?*

In Chapter 6, you learned about demonstrative pronouns **ito** and **nito** (*this*), **iyan** and **niyan** (*that*) and **iyon** and **niyon** (*that,* but farther away from both the speaker and the person addressed). Review what you have learned. What is the difference between **ito** and **nito** (both meaning *this*)? **Ito** is a demonstrative subject pronoun while **nito** is a demonstrative object pronoun.

Another way of looking at the sentence above is to associate **nito** with the meaning "of this." The speaker is saying, "*Do you have something of this in blue?*"

Review how **ito** and **nito** are used in the following sentences.

Blusa ito.	Blouse + this. *This is a blouse.*
Yari sa cotton ito.	Made + of + cotton + this. *This is made of cotton.*
Mayroon akong blusang ito sa asul.	Have + I + **na** + blouse + this + in + blue. *I have this blouse in blue.*
Mayroon ako nito sa asul.	Have + I + this. *I have this in blue.*
Maganda ang kulay ng blouse na ito.	Beautiful + **ang** + color + of blouse + **na** + this. *The color of this blouse is beautiful.*

Maganda ang kulay nito.	Beautiful + **ang** + color + of this.
	Its color is beautiful. / The color of this is beautiful.

In the sentences above, we can learn the following:

1. When using **mayroon** (*have*), always use **nito**, and not **ito**.
   CORRECT: **Mayroon ako nito.** *I have this.*
   WRONG: **Mayroon ako ito.**

2. The word **nito** can be used to indicate possession. In the example below, **nito** is used to mean *of this.*

kulay nitong blusa	color + of this + **na** + blouse.
	color of this blouse

You can say the same thing using **ito**, as in the example below.

kulay ng blusang ito	color + **ng** + blouse + this.
	color of this blouse

Study the following chart of demonstrative subject pronouns and demonstrative object pronouns.

Demonstrative Subject Pronouns	Demonstrative Object Pronouns
ito *this*	**nito** *this, of this*
iyan *that*	**niyan** *that, of that*
iyon *that* (farther away)	**niyon** *that, of that*

Here are a few examples of these pronouns in sentences.

Mayroon ako niyan.	*I have that.*
Maganda ang kulay niyon.	*The color of that is beautiful. /Its color is beautiful.*

CULTURE NOTE (Markets) Although **tiangge** can be loosely translated as a "farmers' market," vendors sell a variety of things, such as produce, baked goods, clothing, handmade jewelry, medicine, books, and even pets. Bargaining is expected. Some malls also have **tiangge**-like spaces, with retailers selling their goods in small stalls.

DIALOGUE PRACTICE

Study the following brief dialogues, all of which express ways to bargain. Note that one dialogue uses Filipino English.

Exchange 1

MELISSA : **May tawad ho ba?** *Is there a discount?*

TINDERA : **Sige ho. Apat na raan na lang.** *Okay. Just four hundred.*

Exchange 2

MELISSA : **Bigyan niyo naman ako ng kaunting tawad.**
Please give me a small discount.

TINDERA : **Pasensiya na kayo. Wala hong tawad dito.** *I am sorry. There is no discount here.*

Exchange 3

MELISSA : **Kaunting discount naman ho.** *Please give me a small discount, please.*

TINDERA : **Ay, sori. Last price na iyan.** *Oh, sorry. That's the final price.*

> **VOCABULARY NOTE** The word **tawad** not only means *discount* but also *forgiveness*. One can say "**Patawad**" or "**Patawarin mo ako**," which is a formal way of saying, "Forgive me."

VOCABULARY PRACTICE

Look at the following pictures. Identify the pieces of clothing.

_____   _____   _____   _____

FINDING THE RIGHT FIT

Now, let us follow Ralph as he goes shopping at a department store. He wants to buy a shirt to wear at the Christmas party. His size is medium, but the medium-sized shirt is too small for him. He wants to try the large-sized shirt.

Let us first study useful words and phrases. You have studied some adjectives in earlier chapters, as well as comparatives. Review these words. In this chapter, focus on expressions such as **napakaliit** or **masyadong maliit** (*too small*), and **napakahaba** or **masyadong mahaba** (*too long*).

Note that when shopping for clothes in department stores, the English terms *small, medium, large, extra small*, and *extra large* are usually used. Number sizes such as 2, 4, 6, 8 may also be used, depending on the manufacturer.

tindero	*male sales clerk*
sukat	*size*
sukatin	*to try on*
Puwede ko bang sukatin ito?	Can + I + **ba** + **na** + try on + this? *Can I try this on?*
maliit	*small*
napakaliit/masyadong maliit	*too small*
palitan	*change, exchange*
Puwede ko ho bang palitan?	Can + I + **ho** + **ba** + **na** + exchange? *Can I exchange this?*

 **DIALOGUE C**

RALPH : **Puwede ko ho bang sukatin ito?** *Can I try this on?*

TINDERO : **Sige ho.** *Okay.*

RALPH : **Napakaliit ho para sa akin. Puwede ko ho bang palitan?** *It is too small for me. Can I exchange it?*

TINDERO : **Heto ho ang Large.** *Here is the Large.*

VOCABULARY

Study these words, and then practice the dialogue again using your own ideas.

masikip	*tight*
napakasikip/masyadong masikip	*too tight*
pinakamaliit	*smallest*
maluwang	*loose*
napakaluwang/masyadong maluwang	*too loose*
maiksi/maikli	*short*
napakaiksi/masyadong maiksi/ napakaikli/masyadong maikli	*too short*
mahaba	*long*
masyadong mahaba/napakahaba	*too long*

GRAMMAR

Adjectives

Review how to form adjectives and adjectival phrases using affixes.

liit	*small* (root word)
maliit	*small*
mas	*more*
mas maliit	*smaller*
pinaka-	*most*
pinakamaliit	*smallest*
napaka-	*too*
napakaliit	*too small*

When using the word **mas** (*more*), put the word before the adjective. For example, **mas + maliit = mas maliit** (*smaller*)

When using the **pinaka-** (*most*) affix, attach the affix to the adjective. For example, **pinaka- + maliit = pinakamaliit** (*smallest*).

However, when using the **napaka-** (*too*) affix, attach the affix to the root word. For example, **napaka- + liit = napakaliit** (*too small*).

CORRECT: **napakaiksi** (*too short*)
WRONG: **napakamaiksi**

Verbs

In this chapter, we are studying two verbs **sukat** (*try on*) and **palit** (*exchange*). The verb **palit** has been introduced in Chapter 9. Study the conjugations of these verbs using the following table.

Root Word	Infinitive/ Imperative	Completed	Incompleted	Contemplated
sukat *try on* (actor focus)	magsukat	nagsukat	nagsusukat	magsusukat
sukat *try on* (object focus)	sukatin	isinukat	isinusukat	isusukat
palit *exchange* (actor focus)	magpalit	nagpalit	nagpapalit	magpapalit
palit *exchange* (directional focus)	palitan	pinalitan	pinapalitan	papalitan
palit *exchange* (causative, causer focus)	magpapalit	nagpapalit	nagpapapalit	magpapapalit
palit *exchange* (causative, directional focus)	papalitan	pinapalitan	pinapapalitan	papapalitan

Study the following words, phrases, and sentences.

nagpalit (*changed, exchanged*)

Nagpalit ako ng blusa.	*I changed my blouse.*
Pinalitan ko ang blusa ko.	*It was my blouse I changed.*
Nagpapalit ako ng blusa sa tindera.	*I asked the salesperson to exchange the blouse.*
Pinapalitan ko ang blusa sa tindera.	*It was a blouse that I asked the sales clerk to exchange.*

DIALOGUE PRACTICE

Create dialogues according to the following situations.

Situation 1 You are in a department store. You want to buy a blouse with a round collar. The blouse is made of silk. You want the blouse in yellow.

You   : **Gusto ko hong** _____.

CLERK : **Ano hong klaseng blusa?**

YOU : _____.

CLERK : **Heto ho.**

YOU : **Ano ho ang telang ito?**

CLERK : **Gawa ho ang blusang ito sa** _____.

YOU : **Mayroon ho ba** _____?

CLERK : **Heto ho.**

Situation 2 You want to try on some pants. However, the pants are too loose for you. You ask the clerk to exchange the pants for a Small.

YOU : **Puwede ko ho** _____?

CLERK : **Sige ho.**

YOU : _____. **Puwede ko ho bang**

_____?

CLERK : **Anong size ho ang gusto niyo?**

YOU : _____.

Situation 3 You want to buy a hat. You ask the clerk how much the hat costs. He tells you that it is one hundred and fifty pesos. You tell him you'll take it. You give him two hundred pesos and he gives you your change.

YOU : _____ **ho ang** _____ **na ito?**

CLERK : **Sandaang piso ho.**

YOU : _____. **Heto ho ang dalawang daang piso.**

CLERK : _____.

At the Party

Melissa and Ralph are at the Christmas party wearing their new clothes. Study greetings and compliments.

Maligayang Pasko!	_Merry Christmas!_
Manigong Bagong Taon!	_Happy New Year!_
Ang ganda ng bestida mo!	**Ang** + beautiful + **ng** + dress + your!
	What a beautiful dress!

nagdala	*brought*
Ikaw ba ang nagdala ng dessert?	You + **ba** + brought + **ng** + dessert? *Did you bring the dessert?*
Ang sarap!	**Ang** + delicious! *It's delicious!*

DIALOGUE D

SARAH : **Maligayang Pasko!** *Merry Christmas!*

MELISSA : **Maligayang Pasko, Ralph!** *Merry Christmas, Ralph!*

RALPH : **Maligayang Pasko at Manigong Bagong Taon! Ang ganda ng bestida mo!** *Merry Christmas and Happy New Year! What a beautiful dress!*

MELISSA : **Salamat.** *Thank you.*

SARAH : **Ikaw ba ang nagdala ng dessert?** *Did you bring the dessert?*

RALPH : **Oo.** *Yes.*

MELISSA : **Ang sarap!** *It's delicious!*

SUMMING UP

In this chapter, we have focused on shopping, clothing vocabulary, and adjectives, and verbs.

Sum up the chapter by talking about Sarah, Melissa and Ralph's experiences. Please complete the paragraphs by writing two or more sentences.

Bumili si Sarah ng blusa. _____

_____

Bumili si Melissa ng bestida. _____.

_____

Nagsukat si Ralph ng pantalon. _____.

_____.

Now write your own paragraph about your recent experience shopping for clothes.

_____

_____

Grammar Index

actor focus, Chapter 7
adjectival affixes,
  Chapter 20
adjectives that describe
  people, Chapter 4
adjectives that describe
  objects, Chapter 6
akin, possessive pronoun,
  Chapter 6
ako, first person pronoun,
  Chapter 1
alin, Chapter 6
-an, affix, directional
  focus, Chapter 13
-an- -in, affix, Chapter 15
ang, marker, Chapter 1

bago (before) and
  pagkatapos (after) with
  verbs, Chapter 11

causative sentences,
  Chapter 10
cause and effect, Chapter 16
comparatives and
  superlatives, Chapter 4
complex sentences,
  Chapter 19
conditionality, Chapter 15
contemplated aspect of
  the verb, Chapter 15

demonstrative pronouns,
  Chapter 6, Chapter 8,
  Chapter 20
directional focus,
  Chapter 9, Chapter 15
din and **rin** usage,
  Chapter 1
**dito/rito/nandito/
  narito**, differences,
  Chapter 5
**diyan/riyan/nandiyan/
  nariyan**, differences,
  Chapter 5

**doon/roon/nandoon/
  naroon**, Lesson 5

expressing action done by
  one person to another,
  Chapter 14

gaano kadalas (how
  often), Chapter 12
gusto, Chapter 7

helping verbs, Chapter 20
honorifics, Chapter 1

i- , affix, Chapter 9
ikaw, second person
  pronoun, Chapter 1
ilan, Chapter 7
-in-, affix, Chapter 20
intensifying adjectives,
  Chapter 13
isa (used for the English
  articles *a/an*), Chapter 2
iyo, second person,
  Chapter 6

ka, second person
  pronoun, Chapter 1
kami, first person
  pronoun, Chapter 1
kanino, Chapter 6
kanya, Chapter 6
kay, Chapter 4, Chapter 6
kayo, second person
  pronoun, Chapter 1
kaysa, comparative usage,
  Chapter 4
ko, first person pronoun,
  Chapter 1, Chapter 6

likes and dislikes, Chapter
  13
linker (**na**) with question
  words, Chapter 2

linking adjectives and
  nouns, Chapter 6

madalas, adverb of
  frequency, Chapter 12
mag-, affix, completed,
  incompleted, and
  contemplative aspects,
  Chapter 2, Chapter 10
magpa-, affix, Chapter 9,
  Chapter 14
mas, comparative usage,
  Chapter 4
masiyadong, intensifying
  adjective, Chapter 13
may, mayroon, meron,
  words that express
  ownership, Chapter 6
mo, second person
  pronoun, Chapter 1,
  Chapter 6

na, linker, Chapter 2,
  Chapter 3
na-, affix, Chapter 10
nag-, affix, Chapter 2
nagpa-, affix, Chapter 10
naka-, affix, Chapter 2
nang and **ng**, Chapter 11
napaka-, affix to
  intensify, Chapter 13
nasa, Chapter 2, Chapter 5
nasaan, Chapter 2,
  Chapter 5
ng, preposition; linker,
  Chapter 3, Chapter 13
ni, possessive marker,
  Chapter 3
niya, third person
  pronoun, Chapter 1,
  Chapter 6
noon (in the past) and
  ngayon (now),
  Chapter 2

object focus, Chapter 7
ownership words,
    Chapter 7

pa-, affix, Chapter 7,
    saying "please,"
    Chapter 13
pa- -an, affix, Chapter 9
paki-, affix, Chapter 10
palagi, adverb of
    frequency, Chapter 12
paminsan-minsan,
    adverb of frequency,
    Chapter 12
pina-, affix, Chapter 14
pina- -an, affix, Chapter 9
pinaka-, Chapter 4
possessive pronouns and
    adjectives, Chapter 6

pronouns, Chapter 1,
    Chapter 4, Chapter 6
puwede, Chapter 7

sa, Chapter 2;
    comparative usage,
    Chapter 4, Chapter 6
saan, Chapter 2
sentence construction,
    Chapter 1, Chapter 2
si, marker, Chapter 1,
    Chapter 3
sila, third person
    pronoun, Chapter 1
siya, third person
    pronoun, Chapter 1
special verbs, Chapter 3

tayo, first person

pronoun, Chapter 1

um-, affix, Chapter 2,
    Chapter 10, Chapter 11,
    Chapter 18

verbs and root words,
    Chapter 3
verb aspects, Chapter 2,
    Chapter 3
verb conjugations,
    Chapter 8, Chapter 12,
    Chapter 18
verb conjugations, special
    rules, Chapter 17
verb focus, Chapter 7

yes or no questions and
    use of **ba**, Chapter 8

English–Tagalog Glossary

6:00 a.m. **alas-sais ng
    umaga/ika-anim ng
    umaga**
7:00 a.m. **alas-siyete ng
    umaga/ika-pito ng
    umaga**
8:00 a.m. **alas-otso ng
    umaga/ika-walo ng
    umaga**

above/top part **nasa itaas**
according to **ayon sa**
advance **paunang bayad**
affix; please **paki-**
after **makalipas,
    pagkatapos**
after eating **pagkatapos
    kumain**
after my class
    pagkatapos ng klase ko
again **uli**
airplane **eroplano**
alley **iskinita**

already **na**
also/too **din/rin**
always **palagi**
American **Amerikano**
anniversary **anibersaryo**
another slice **isa pang
    slice**
answer **sagutan**
April **Abril**
architect **arkitekto**
arm **braso**
around **bandang**
(to) arrive **darating**
arriving **dumarating**
ask to buy **pabili**
at noon **ng tanghali**
ate **kumain**
attend **dadalo**
August **Agosto**

back **likod**
banca (small boat)
    bangka

bank manager **manedyer
    ng bangko**
baptism **binyag**
bathroom **banyo**
beautiful (used for men)
    guwapo/makisig
beautiful (used for
    women) **maganda**
(to) become **maging**
bed **kama**
bedroom/room **kuwarto**
beef **baka**
before **bago**
before reaching **bago
    umabot**
before sleeping **bago
    matulog**
below/lower part **nasa
    ibaba**
belt **sinturon**
beside **katabi**
bicycle **bisikleta**
big/large **malaki**

bitter **mapait**
black **itim**
bland **matabang**
blood **dugo**
blouse **blusa**
boiled **nilaga**
boiled beef **nilagang baka**
book **libro**
bowl **mangkok**
breakfast **almusal**
bright **maliwanag**
bringing/brought
(literally, have bring)
may dala
British **Briton** (people)
broth **sabaw**
brother/sister **kapatid**
brother-in-law **bayaw**
brown **kayumanggi/
kulay kape**
brushes teeth
nagsesepilyo
bus **bus**
business person
negosyante
busy **abala**
buy **bili**

calendar **kalendaryo**
(will) call **tatawagan**
called **tumawag**
can get **puwedeng
makuha**
Can I ask a question?
**Puwede ba akong
magtanong?**
Can I ask? **Puwede ba
akong humingi?**
Can I try on? **Puwede
ko bang sukatin?**
can/may **puwede**
car **kotse**
cents **sentimos**
chair **silya**
chest/breast **dibdib**
chicken **manok**

chicken stewed in vinegar
adobong manok
China **Tsina**
Chinese **Tsino/Tsina**
citizen **mamamayan**
city **lungsod**
cleans **naglilinis**
clock **orasan**
close/near **malapit**
clothing **damit**
cold **malamig**
collar **kuwelyo**
come on/please **sige na**
coming from **galing sa**
complete name/full name
buong pangalan
computer **kompyuter**
(to) confirm
kumpirmahin
continent **kontinente**
cooks **nagluluto**
corner **kanto**
cost **halaga**
cotton **bulak**
cough **ubo**
count **bilang**
country **bansa**
cup **tasa**

daily **araw-araw**
dances **sumasayaw**
dark **madilim**
dawn **madaling-araw**
December **Disyembre**
delicious **masarap**
denim pants **maong**
(to) depart/leave **aalis**
deposit **deposito**
dessert **panghimagas**
dining room **komedor/
silid-kainan**
dinner **hapunan**
(will) do **gagawin**
Do you have this in...?
**Mayroon ba kayo nito
sa...?**

Do you know...? **Alam
mo ba...?**
doctor **doktor**
dollars **dolyar**
don't **huwag**
drank **uminom**
dress **bestida**
dress (refers only to a
woman's one-piece
dress) **bestida**
dresses up **nagbibihis**
drink **inumin/maiinom**
drink **inom** (root word)
driver **drayber**
driving **nagmamaneho**

ear **tenga**
early **maaga**
eat **kainin**
eat **kain** (root word)
eight **walo**
eight o'clock **alas-otso**
eighteen **labingwalo**
eighty **walumpu**
elder brother **kuya**
elder sister **ate**
electric fan **bentilador**
eleven **labing-isa**
eleven o'clock **alas-onse**
employee **kawani**
engineer **inhinyero**
English **Ingles**
(to) escort/go with
sumabay
ethnicity **etnisidad**
every **tuwing**
every[day] at seven o'clock
tuwing alas-siyete
exactly at noon
tanghaling tapat
(to) exchange money;
have money **magpapalit**
exchange rate **palitan**
exercises (referring to
physical exercise)
nag-eehersisyo

expression equivalent to "oh" **naku**

eye **mata**

fabric/cloth **tela**

fall **taglagas**

fan **pamaypay**

far **malayo**

fare **pamasahe**

farmer **magsasaka**

farther away **mas malayo**

farthest **pinakamalayo**

fast **mabilis**

February **Pebrero**

feet **paa**

fifteen **labinlima**

fifty **limampu**

fine **mabuti**

finger **daliri**

fireman **bumbero**

first person singular **ako**

first person singular, possessive **ko**

fish **isda**

five **lima**

five o'clock **alas-singko**

flu **trankaso**

food **pagkain**

fork **tinidor**

forty **apatnapu**

four **apat**

four o'clock **alas-kuwatro**

fourteen **labing-apat**

Friday **Biyernes**

fried **prito**

fried fish **pritong isda**

friendly **palakaibigan**

from **mula**

from (literally, from-where) **taga-saan**

from Los Angeles **taga-Los Angeles**

from, with **galing** (accent on the first syllable)

full **busog**

funeral **libing**

garage **garahe**

garden **hardin**

get **makuha**

(to) get off **bababa**

glass **baso**

Go around the Rotonda! **Umikot ka sa Rotonda!**

Go back to the Faculty Center! **Bumalik ka sa Faculty Center!**

Go past the movie theater! **Lumampas ka ng sinehan!**

Go straight! **Dumiretso ka!**

go to class **pumasok sa klase** (literally, enter class)

go with; join **sumama**

go, come **punta**

goes around **namamasyal**

goes home **umuuwi**

goes to (class/work) **pumapasok**

going to **papuntang**

gold **kulay ginto**

good **mabait**

Good afternoon! **Magandang hapon!**

Good day! **Magandang araw!**

Good evening! **Magandang gabi!**

Good morning! **Magandang umaga!**

Good noon! **Magandang tanghali!**

got broken (for example, an arm or a leg) **nabali**

got burned **napaso/ nasunog**

government employee **kawani ng gobyerno**

graduation **pagtatapos**

grandchild **apo**

grandfather **lolo**

grandmother **lola**

Great Britain **Inglatera**

green **luntian/berde**

gray **kulay abo**

grilled/roasted **inihaw**

grilled/roasted chicken **inihaw na manok**

grouchy **masungit**

hair **buhok**

half (used for thirty minutes) **y medya**

hand **kamay**

handkerchief **panyo**

hard-working **masipag**

has a collar **may kuwelyo/may collar**

has a round collar **may collar na pabilog**

has a V neckline **V ang neckline**

hat **sumbrero**

have a party/will party **makakapag-party**

have something examined **magpa-eksamen**

have you seen **nakita**

have your x-rays taken **magpa-xray**

having diarrhea **nagtatae**

head **pinuno**

heads (used as a verb) **namumuno**

heart **puso**

helpful **matulungin**

here **dito/rito/nandito/ narito**

here it is... **heto**

hips **balakang**

hold a meeting **magpupulong**

honey **honey**

hope **sana**

hot **mainit**

house **bahay**

how **paano**

how [are you] related to **kaano-ano**
How are you? (informal; casual) **Kumusta ka?**
how many **ilan**
How many rooms (are there)? **Ilan ho ang kuwarto?**
how much **gaano karami**
how much **magkano**
how often **gaano kadalas**
how/that is how **ganun/ ganoon**
hungry **gutom**

I hope to **gusto ko sana**
I want to buy **gusto ko hong bumili**
I want to open **gusto ko hong magbukas**
I want to rent **gusto ko hong umupa**
I will find out... **aalamin ko ho; titingnan ko ho**
if **kung**
if it's possible/if it's okay. **kung puwede....**
in front **nasa harap**
in front of **tapat/sa tapat**
in the afternoon **ng hapon**
in the evening **ng gabi**
in the future **sa hinaharap**
in the morning **ng umaga**
in the past **noon**
included **kasama**
in-law **manugang**
inside/in **nasa loob**
intelligent **matalino**
interview **interbyu**
Is that so? **Ganoon ba?**
island **isla**

it is somewhere around... **nasa bandang**
It's delicious! **Ang sarap!**

January **Enero**
Japan **Hapon**
Japanese **Hapon/ Haponesa**
jeepney; a custom-made Filipino vehicle made from surplus US army jeeps **dyipni**
join **sasama**
juice **katas/dyus/juice**
July **Hulyo**
June **Hunyo**
just **lang**
just ride with me in my car **sumakay ka na sa akin sa kotse ko**

key **susi**
kitchen **kusina**
knee **tuhod**
knife **kutsilyo**

large **malaki**
large ship **barko**
late **huli** (pronounced with accent on the last syllable)
lawyer **abugado**
leave **alis**
lemon **limon**
Light Rail Transit **LRT**
liquor; alcohol **alak**
(will) listen to music **makikinig ng musika**
literature **panitikan**
living in (referring to place of residence) **nakatira**
living room **sala**
long **mahaba**
long-sleeved **mahaba ang manggas**

looking for **hinahanap** (object focus), **naghahanap** (subject focus)
loose **maluwang**
low **mababa**
lower **mas mababa**
lowest **pinakamababa**
lunch **tanghalian**

made in/made of **gawa sa/yari sa**
March **Marso**
mathematics **matematika**
May **Mayo**
meat and vegetables in peanut sauce **kare-kare**
(to) meet **makilala**
(to) meet up **magtagpo**
(to) meet; (to) see each other **magkita**
meeting (noun); as in a group meeting **pulong**
Metro Rail Transit **MRT**
midnight **hatinggabi**
milk **gatas**
milk custard **leche flan**
minute **minuto**
moderate **katamtaman**
Monday **Lunes**
most beautiful **pinakamaganda**
mouth **bibig**

narrow **makitid**
nationality **nasyonalidad**
native lemon **kalamansi**
nearer/closer **mas malapit**
nearest/closest **pinakamalapit**
(to) need **kailangan**
never **hindi kailanman**
news **balita**

next **susunod**
next Saturday **susunod**
  na Sabado
niece/nephew
  pamangkin
nine **siyam**
nine o'clock **alas-nuwebe**
nineteen **labinsiyam**
ninety **siyamnapu**
no collar **walang**
  kuwelyo
noodle **pansit**
notebook **kuwaderno**
November **Nobyembre**
now **ngayon**
nurse **nars**

October **Oktubre**
of course **siyempre**
often **madalas**
okay **sige**
old **matanda**
on the right **nasa**
  kanan...
on the side of **nasa tabi**
on top of **nasa ibabaw**
one **isa**
one billion **isang bilyon**
one hundred **sandaan**
one hundred thousand
  sandaang libo
one million **isang**
  milyon
one moment **sandali**
  lang
one o'clock **ala-una**
one thousand **sanlibo**
onions **sibuyas**
(to) open **magbukas**
orange **kulay kahel**
order **orderin**
outside **nasa labas**
over there **doon/roon/**
  nandoon/naroon

pants **pantalon**

paper **papel**
(will) pass by; (will) pick
  up [someone]
  dadaanan
(to) pay **magbayad**
payment **bayad**
pencil **lapis**
perhaps **siguro**
permanent **permanente**
peso (referring to the
  Philippine peso) **piso**
pet **alagang hayop**
pet cat **alagang pusa**
pet dog **alagang aso**
Philippine literature
  panitikang Filipino
Philippine society
  lipunang Filipino
phone **telepono**
pink **kulay rosas**
place of meeting
  tagpuan
plans will push through
  matutuloy ang plano
plate **plato**
(will) play (a game)
  maglalaro
(will) play (a musical
  instrument) **tutugtog**
(will) play golf **maggo-**
  golf
(will) play the guitar
  tutugtog ng gitara
plays soccer **nagsasoccer**
plays tennis **nagtetennis**
please answer
  pakisagutan
please count **pakibilang**
please give (us)
  pakibigyan
please sign
  pakipirmahan
pleased **ikinagagalak**
police officer **pulis**
polo shirt **shirt**
poor **mahirap**

pork in sour broth
  sinigang na baboy
possessive marker **ni**
practices (for example,
  practices a musical
  instrument or a sport)
  nag-eensayo
practices yoga **nagyoyoga**
practicing **nagpapraktis**
preposition: in, on; at
  nasa
preposition: in/on/at/
  during **sa**
preposition; linker **ng**
proof **pruweba**
proof of residence
  pruweba ng tirahan
province **probinsiya**
public transportation
  pampublikong
  transportasyon
purple/violet/ lavender
  lila

question **tanong**

race **lahi**
rain **ulan**
(will) rain **uulan**
rainy **maulan**
rainy or wet season
  tag-ulan
rarely **bihira**
reads **nagbabasa**
really **talaga**
red **pula**
researcher **mananaliksik**
residence **tirahan**
rest **magpahinga**
rice **kanin**
rice noodles **bihon**
rich **mayaman**
(to) ride/get on **sasakay**
riding a bicycle
  nagbibisikleta
road **kalsada**

road, pass **daan**
runny nose **sipon**
runs **tumatakbo**
Russia **Rusya**
Russian **Ruso**

salad **ensalada**
salmon in sour broth
  sinigang na salmon
salty **maalat**
sandals **sandalyas**
Saturday **Sabado**
sauteed **guisado**
sauteed rice noodles
  **guisadong pansit
  bihon**
science **siyensiya**
second (time) **segundo**
second person singular **ka**
(to) see **makita**
separate **hiwalay**
September **Setyembre**
(to) set up **mag-set**
seven **pito**
seven o'clock **alas-siyete**
seventeen **labimpito**
seventy **pitumpu**
shoes **sapatos**
shops **namimili**
short **maikli/maiksi**
should **dapat**
shoulder **balikat**
sign **karatula**
silk **seda/sutla**
silver **kulay pilak**
sings **kumakanta**
sister-in law **bilas**
six **anim**
six o'clock **alas-sais**
sixteen **labing-anim**
sixty **animnapu**
size **sukat**
skin **balat**
skirt **palda**
sleeveless **walang
  manggas**

slow **mabagal**
small **maliit**
small plate; saucer
  platito
smaller **mas maliit**
smallest **pinakamaliit**
smallest political unit in the
  Philippines **barangay**
snack **merienda**
So sweet! **Ang tamis!**
society **lipunan**
sofa **sofa**
sometimes **minsan/
  paminsan-minsan**
soup **sopas**
Spain **Espanya**
Spaniard **Kastila**
spicy **maanghang**
spoon **kutsara**
spring **tagsibol**
state **estado**
steamed **pinasingaw**
steamed vegetables
  pinasingaw na gulay
stomach **tiyan**
Stop! **Huminto ka!**
storm **bagyo**
stormy **bumabagyo**
street **kalye**
student **estudyante**
studied for a master's
  degree **nag-master's**
studying **nag-aaral**
sugar **asukal**
summer (also dry season)
  tag-araw
sun (another meaning of
  araw is "day") **araw**
Sunday **Linggo**
sunny **maaraw**
sweet **matamis**

table **mesa**
tablet **tabletas**
take (literally, drink)
  inumin

take these tablets
  **inumin mo ang mga
  tabletas na ito**
take vitamins **uminom
  ng bitamina**
takes a bath/shower
  naliligo/nagsa-shower
taking a vacation
  nagbabakasyon
talkative **madaldal**
tall (used for people)
  matangkad
taller **mas matangkad**
tallest **pinakamatangkad**
tangy **mapakla**
tasty **malasa**
taxi **taksi**
teacher **guro/titser**
teeth **ngipin**
ten **sampu**
ten o'clock **alas-diyes**
ten thousand **sampung
  libo**
that (closer to the person
  addressed) **iyan**
that (far from both the
  speaker and the person
  addressed) **iyon**
the exchange rate is high
  mataas ang palitan
the exchange rate is
  higher **mas mataas
  ang palitan**
the exchange rate is
  highest **pinakamataas
  ang palitan**
there **diyan/riyan/
  nandiyan/nariyan**
there are two rooms
  **may dalawang
  kuwarto**
there is **may/mayroon**
thick **makapal**
thin (only to objects, not
  people) **manipis**
thirteen **labintatlo**

thirty **tatlumpu**
this **ito**
this is… **ito si**
three **tatlo**
three o'clock **alas-tres**
three times a day
tatlong beses isang
throat **lalamunan**
Thursday **Huwebes**
ticket **tiket**
tight **masikip**
time; hour **oras**
to/until **hanggang**
tomato and onion salad
ensaladang kamatis at sibuyas
tomatoes **kamatis**
too bitter **masyadong mapait**
too long **masyadong mahaba/napakahaba**
too loose
napakaluwang/ masyadong maluwang
too short **napakaiksi/ masyadong maiksi/ napakaikli/masyadong maikli**
too small **napakaliit/ masyadong maliit**
too tight **napakasikip/ masyadong masikip**
town; country; people
bayan
train **tren**
travel **biyahe**
traveling **pagbibiyahe**
tricycle (a motorcycle or a bicycle with a sidecar)
traysikel
truck **trak**
try on **sukatin**
t-shirt **t-shirt**
Tuesday **Martes**
Turn left! **Kumaliwa ka!**
Turn right! **Kumanan ka!**

twelve **labindalawa**
twelve o'clock **alas-dose**
twenty **dalawampu**
twenty-one
dalawampu't isa
twenty-two
dalawampu't dalawa
two **dalawa**
two o'clock **alas-dos**
type of blouse **klase ng blusa**

ugly **pangit**
umbrella **payong**
uncle **tiyo/tiyuhin/tito**
under **nasa ilalim**
United States **Estados Unidos**
universe **kalawakan/ uniberso**
used to mean "still";
another/more **pa**
used when the focus is on the doer of the action
mag

vegetables **gulay**
very bitter **napakapait/ mapait na mapait**
very hungry **gutom na gutom**
very sour **napakaasim**
vomiting **nagsusuka**

waist **baywang**
waiting **naghihintay**
walk **lakad**
walking **naglalakad**
wallet **pitaka**
was infected **nahawa**
was wounded
nasugatan
washes one's face
naghihilamos
watch **relo**

(will) watch television
manonood ng telebisyon
water **tubig**
water bottle **bote ng tubig**
weather **panahon**
wedding **kasal**
Wednesday **Miyerkules**
what **ano**
When can I move in/ transfer? **Kailan ako puwedeng lumipat?**
where **nasaan/ saan**
Where are you going?
Saan ka pupunta?
white **puti**
who **sino**
why **bakit**
wide **malapad**
wind **hangin**
winds are strong
malakas ang hangin
windy **mahangin**
winter **taglamig**
woke up **gumising**
worker **manggagawa**
working **nagtatrabaho**
world **daigdig/ mundo**
writer **manunulat**

yellow **dilaw**
yet; expression used to mean "first" or "to do"
muna
you (second person, plural for honorific)
kayo
you want/would like to eat **gusto mong kainin**
you want/would like to order **gusto niyong orderin**
young **bata**
younger **mas bata**